Self-Rescue

A CHOCKSTONE PRESS BOOK

FALCON®

HELENA, MONTANA

David J. Fasulo
how to rock climb series

SELF-RESCUE

FRONT COVER:
Craig Yaw on the North Ridge of Mt. Stewart, Washington, Cascades. Photo: Jim Dockery.

All illustrations by Mike Clelland.

ISBN 0-934641-97-8

PUBLISHED AND DISTRIBUTED BY:
Falcon Press Publishing Co, Inc.
P.O. Box 1718
Helena, Montana 59624

Letters to the author are welcome. Enclose a self-addressed, stamped envelope and mail comments to David Fasulo c/o Falcon Press.

C O N T E N T S

SELF-
RESCUE

DAVID J. FASULO

Forward

Anyone who climbs very often or for very long must expect sooner or later to be involved in misfortune, if not his own, then someone else's.
—Mountaineering: Freedom of the Hills

Despite all of the technological and psychological advances in mountaineering during recent years, the sport and its many disciplines (e.g. technical rock and ice climbing, extreme skiing, etc.) is still an inherently dangerous activity. The number of reported accidents per year in the United States ranges from 130 to 200, including up to 50 deaths, and a majority of climbing accidents, consisting of minor injuries and near misses, go unreported.

Advances in rescue and emergency medicine, coupled with an increase in the number of rescue teams and faster access to wilderness areas, have in some ways caused climbers to tone down on their traditional self-reliance. However, the importance of providing quality first aid during the "golden hour" (the first hour following a life-threatening accident) and the remote locations of both old and new fashionable climbing areas should prompt climbers to be prepared for any possibility. Emergency preparedness becomes even more critical for those undertaking expeditions to Third World countries, where medical care is poor and rescue non-existent.

Preplanning for emergencies by recreational climbers is very difficult because the underlying attitude is to have fun. No one plans a climb to purposely get injured, lost, killed or rescued. Accepting these possibilities, however, is one of the most important aspects of developing a good safety attitude. And the best way to deal with these possibilities is to have an emergency plan laid out before ever leaving home.

There are numerous aspects to developing a good emergency plan. First and foremost is establishing safe and reasonable goals for the climbing party that will sufficiently challenge yet allow for a margin of safety, if not total success. Consider the difficulty of the goal, the amount of time allotted, the complexity of the approach, the details of the descent route, and match this with the experience and fitness of all party members, as well as the availability of the proper equipment.

Many accidents happen to climbers in their "storm years," those three years or so after most have passed through the beginner stage and are testing themselves without complete knowledge of what they are getting into. Experience does not come overnight and it is sometimes earned at too high a price.

Another aspect of the emergency plan is checking the condition of all ropes, technical equipment and other gear and clothing well in advance of leaving home. In particular, ropes should be checked every time they are recoiled.

Keeping a log of an individual rope's use is helpful, even if only serving as a reminder of how old or how much stress it has accumulated. Organize your equipment before a climb, and make sure first aid and other essential items are easy to access.

Certain equipment should always be carried. This includes a first-aid kit (don't go robbing it of essential medical tape to tape hands for rock climbing!), short prusik slings and extra carabiners on your harness, a headlamp or flashlight with fresh batteries, extra food and water, change for a pay phone, and a signaling device, such as mirror or smoke device. You also should carry a stuff sack packed with storm clothing appropriate for survival in the particular climbing area and season of your trip. The choice of items for, and the size of the first-aid kit will depend upon the owner's level of first aid certification, personal choices and local climactic considerations. For instance, heat packs may be indispensable for a winter first-aid kit in the northern Rockies, but the snake-bite kit and malaria meds may be left at home!

The final step in wrapping up preparations before each individual trip is to leave a trip plan with a responsible friend or relative, as well as contact phone numbers for the appropriate rescue or law enforcement agency, and directions on how to utilize such information. Many mountaineers give themselves a buffer zone – an acceptable late-arrival period – beyond when they would ideally like to return home, as often minor complications become time-costly, but not dangerous, during a climb. Agency contact information, emergency notification procedures and hospital locations should be given to all members of the climbing party.

The most important part of emergency planning is education. This is a life-long process of continual review and practice. One may pursue a combination of self-study with books and videos, formal course work, practice with partners or local clubs, and membership and/or volunteer work with local rescue and emergency medicine agencies. Recommended topics to pursue include safety courses in climbing techniques, emergency medical certifications (e.g. cardiopulmonary resuscitation, advanced first aid, etc.), rescue training (various regional and seasonal topics), outdoor leadership skills, meteorology, orienteering and foreign languages (if considering a foreign expedition).

Physical conditioning is just about as important as mental conditioning. Formulate a training program and stick to it. Books and local experts will help if you need support. Stay fit!

Emergency planning is a multi-faceted process with both long-term and short-term goals. It should not involve paranoia but rather a logical, common sense approach to avoiding a rescue. It can also make a critical difference on inevitable or unavoidable disasters.

JIM DETTERLINE

Climbing Ranger
Rocky Mountain National Park

Preface

Sometimes a little knowledge is dangerous. Although I believe there is a need for self-rescue awareness, attempting some of the skills described in this book without adequate practice, in adverse conditions, or without adequate experience in the basics of rock climbing may lead to serious injuries or death.

Furthermore, certain injuries or complicated rescues may require trained rescue personnel with proper equipment. Whatever the situation, your goal is to prevent endangering lives or further complicating your predicament.

Remember, the most important self-rescue skill is the ability to prevent the need for a rescue.

How To Rock Climb: Self-Rescue is designed to provide an academic framework for basic self-rescue techniques. These skills are described in a step-by-step format that provides a clear sequence. This book should be used as a reference; it is not a substitute for a hands-on course in self-rescue.

Furthermore, many of the illustrations have been streamlined for clarity. For example, many of the anchor/belay systems have been simplified so the illustrations won't appear cluttered, and to allow clear depiction of the self-rescue concepts being described. Also, I have chosen the Figure Eight as the backup knot for all the scenarios presented. A Munter Mule knot may be a better choice in some instances because it can be released when loaded. However, if you have not practiced these knots and systems, and you are battling adverse conditions, the likelihood of tying the Munter Mule knot incorrectly is greater than that of botching a Figure Eight. Since the backup knot is so critical, I have chosen to illustrate what I believe is a safer alternative. Please refer to the text as well as the illustrations prior to practicing the self-rescue skills described herein.

If you must use any of the self-rescue skills described in this manual in a real-life situation, you must be absolutely confident in your abilities and the reliability of your anchors. For example, some of the sequences described in the Leader Rescue and The Complete Self-Rescue sections ask you to judge whether the top anchor is completely reliable, even though you would be unable to make a close-up visual inspection. If you are the least bit unsure of the safety or reliability of the rescue system, do not engage the system.

Practicing these skills can be very dangerous! Always use an independent safety line and belayer to ensure your safety.

I would also encourage all readers interested in developing self-rescue skills to read more on the subject and to take a course from a qualified professional. A list of resources is provided in the appendix.

Acknowledgements

The following people have my sincere thanks for their help: Michael Kodas, Ann Parmenter, Mike Clelland, C.M.R., Nick Yardley, Jim Woodmency, Tim Jones, Jim Detterline, Tracy Salcedo, S. Peter Lewis and Jim Dockery. For Lisa and Kyle.

WARNING: CLIMBING IS A SPORT WHERE YOU MAY BE SERIOUSLY INJURED OR DIE

READ THIS BEFORE YOU USE THIS BOOK.

This is an instruction book to rock climbing, a sport which is inherently dangerous. You should not depend solely on information gleaned from this book for your personal safety. Your climbing safety depends on your own judgment based on competent instruction, experience, and a realistic assessment of your climbing ability.

There is no substitute for personal instruction in rock climbing and climbing instruction is widely available. You should engage an instructor or guide to learn climbing safety techniques. If you misinterpret a concept expressed in this book, you may be killed or seriously injured as a result of the misunderstanding. Therefore, the information provided in this book should be used only to supplement competent personal instruction from a climbing instructor or guide. Even after you are proficient in climbing safely, occasional use of a climbing guide is a safe way to raise your climbing standard and learn advanced techniques.

There are no warranties, either expressed or implied, that this instruction book contains accurate and reliable information. There are no warranties as to fitness for a particular purpose or that this book is merchantable. Your use of this book indicates your assumption of the risk of death or serious injury as a result of climbing's risks and is an acknowledgement of your own sole responsibility for your climbing safety.

Introduction

The self-rescue skills presented in this book are designed to help a climber manage difficulties while rescuing victims in technical climbing terrain. The recommended skills require minimal equipment and assistance. However, the ability to perform these skills requires expert rope management.

The recommended techniques and sequences have many variations that are used depending on how much speed is necessary, safety margins, available equipment and personal preference. Regardless of the variation, the principles of *loading* (weighting) and unloading ropes, providing system back-ups and preventing further injuries are the foundation for the techniques presented.

It can be difficult to decide whether to rescue yourself, rely on others for assistance, or combine efforts. You should consider your predicament, resources and abilities. Preventing further or potential injuries to others is the most important aspect to consider before attempting a rescue.

"You are your own best means of rescue with injuries or potential hypothermia," states Jim Woodmency, a ranger at Grand Teton National Park. "You, including the rest of your party or partner, should do everything possible to get out on your own without help. Too many times I've seen people panic and leave a partner to get 'help,' or give up trying to help themselves and just start yelling, when they likely could have extricated themselves from their predicament.

"However, in this day and age, and with the advent of the cellular phone, it is now possible to do both – go for help and help yourself at the same time."

RESCUE PREVENTION

or How Did I Get Myself Into This Mess?

I became interested in self-rescue techniques in 1988. This was the year my partner rescued me off the *Regular Route* on the northwest face of Half Dome in Yosemite.

Craig, my partner, and I drove across country from Connecticut to climb on the big stone in Yosemite. On the way out we did some climbing in Eldorado Canyon. In Estes Park, I led every pitch of the *Casual Route* (V 5.10) on the Diamond, Longs Peak. At Devil's Tower, I was flashing 5.10 and 5.11 on the lead. Physically, I felt prepared.

When we arrived in the Valley, we decided to brush up on aid climbing. We hiked up the Yosemite Falls Trail and I led the *Lost Arrow Tip*. The wild and airy Tyrolean traverse back to the main wall gave us a good introduction to the exposure we came to the Valley to experience. I was totally motivated to tackle Half Dome.

(page opposite)
The higher you climb, the more important your self-rescue skills.

Jim Detterline photo

Working toward the
summit.

Jim Detterline photo

Our plan was to hike to the base, haul a large bag and bivy on the sixth pitch that same day. We hiked up the eight-mile approach trail but ended up retracing much of our hike back to the spring because we'd received erroneous information on water sources. We ended up carrying all of our water back to the base. I was so anxious about getting to the sixth pitch that day, I barely ate or drank anything to save time. We had left very early that morning, and because of the water snafu, didn't arrive at the start of the climb until late in the day.

I led the first pitch and hauled the haul bag, a huge duffel bag, to the belay ledge. The haul bag got stuck a little, but I was able to pull it free. I led the second pitch and then battled with the haul bag. The last few tugs to bring the bag to the sloping ledge required all the strength I could muster.

I had pushed very hard that day, the haul bag was wasting me, and I was so excited about the idea of climbing Half Dome that I didn't realize I needed to pace myself.

Just after the bag reached the second belay, my body began to shake violently. Craig arrived at the ledge, and I tried to say something, but I couldn't speak! While Craig was trying to figure out what the problem was, my eyes involuntarily closed. I was conscious of my surroundings, but unable to move.

I thought about my predicament and would have laughed had my body let me. Let me see, I thought, I'm eight miles from the trailhead, two pitches up the northwest face of Half Dome in a semi-hanging belay. I'm blind and I can't speak. I would have never guessed this is how my day would turn out.

Again I tried to speak, and with my best effort I made a jumbled noise that sounded like "opple." I didn't know why, but I was trying to say apple. I was lucky my partner had just come from a National Outdoor Leadership School course in which he'd received the First Responder Certification. Somehow he figured out I was trying to say apple and recognized what the problem was – hypoglycemic shock.

Craig immediately began to rummage through the haul bag for food and water. He began to feed me chocolate chips from a bag of granola and, after a short time, my eyelids slowly opened. Craig managed to lower me and the haul bag to the ground. We broke open some more food and in a short time I was able to speak.

When I returned home I saw a doctor and he informed me, after testing, that I did not have hypoglycemia or diabetes. I had simply pushed too hard without taking in food or water – without considering the logistics of a big wall.

As this story illustrates, *the most important self-rescue skill is the ability to prevent the need for a rescue.* Since the Half Dome experience, I have been very careful to plan for logistics such as approach time, food, water and weather. The following year, I became certified as a Wilderness First Responder and began guiding part-time. In 1990, I completed a three-day rock rescue course for guides presented by the American Mountain Guide Association. Since this time, I have continued to review literature concerning self-rescue as well as upgrade my first aid training to the EMT level—all for the sake of prevention.

During your travels to the hills, you may encounter life-threatening medical emergencies. I strongly recommend that any backcountry traveler complete a First Responder or Emergency Medical Technician course, as well as a course on self-rescue. These skills may someday save a life.

I eventually climbed the *Regular Route* on the northwest face of Half Dome in two days. Without incident.

The Six Steps of Self-Rescue

Prior to taking any action in a technical rescue situation, follow these six steps to prevent further injuries or complications:

- Survey the scene (i.e., prevent further injuries by identifying potential environmental or other risks to the rescuer, victim or bystanders);

- Determine first aid needs;

- Plan your course of action;

- Build the rescue system;

- Double-check the system;

- Initiate your plan (i.e., administer first aid, self-rescue and/or locate assistance).

(page opposite)

Route finding is an important skill for rescue prevention.

Jim Detterline photo

Equipment should always be in perfect condition before use. Even so, it may suffer damage. Here, a piece of falling sandstone has sliced a rope on Castleton Tower in Utah. Rockfall is a hazard that can be minimized through choice of route and time of day.

Jim Detterline photo

Tools for Self-Rescue

This chapter provides a brief list of the tools you might find useful during a self-rescue. You should have most of these items with you every time you climb.

Accessory Cord

The standard diameter is six or seven millimeters. The diameter of the cord should be smaller than the rope you will be locking or ascending. To form a Prusik loop, I use three- and four-foot lengths tied into a loop with a Double Fisherman's knot.

Never trust an accessory cord alone. Always have a reliable backup in case the cord breaks.

Carabiners

Standard oval or D carabiners are best for rescue. Whenever working with a carabiner, keep in mind that it is not fail-safe. Points to remember with regard to carabiners:

- A carabiner can break if loaded improperly.
- A rope can unclip from a single non-locking carabiner or unlocked locking carabiner.
- Carabiners may be damaged when shock-loaded – the body may elongate if the gate opens during loading. If the body is stretched the gate will not close properly.

These situations may seem unlikely, however I have had carabiners elongate enough to prevent the gate from closing twice during leader falls. I also witnessed a friend fall 40 feet because a carabiner broke during a leader fall. Consider these risks before you lower someone off a single carabiner. If you must trust a life to a single carabiner, inspect it carefully.

Cordelette

When climbing multi-pitch routes, climbers should carry two cordelettes. A cordelette is a 17-foot length of seven-millimeter accessory cord tied into a loop. However, modern fibers offer higher strength in smaller diameter cores. For example, 5.5mm Blue Water Titan Cord is tested at 2200kg. while standard 7mm accessory cord tests at 900 kg. Obviously, the 5.5mm Titan Cord is better suited, though because of it's slippery nature should be tied with a double or triple fishermans knot.

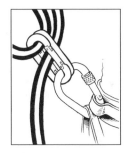

Oval or D carabiners are best for rescue.

Using a cordelette can simplify many of the systems that are described in this book. Unfortunately, the cordelette has not yet become a standard piece of equipment on most climbers' racks. Therefore, many of the skills described in this book incorporate the standard Prusik length of three- and four-foot lengths tied into a loop, instead of the cordelette.

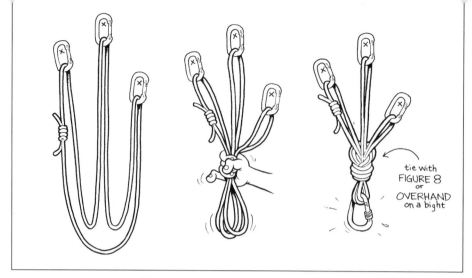

tie with
FIGURE 8
or
OVERHAND
on a bight

Harness

The swami belt is the main component of any climbing harness. Leg loops distribute the climber's weight and add comfort. When connecting to belay anchors, always clip in to the front of your harness. It is difficult to manage a loaded rope, or escape a belay, if the anchor is connected to the back of your harness.

Rope

In most rescue situations, your rope is your path of escape. However, it also can trap a climber who cannot escape from a belay or disconnect a loaded rope from an anchor. Careless rope management may result in a damaged rope, making escape more dangerous or impossible.

Anticipate how to best use your rope during a rescue using the appropriate knots, tools and techniques. Be aware of the path your rope is traveling and conditions that may damage it. Care must be taken to prevent jamming the rope during rappels. Avoid damaging your rope by padding sharp edges. Ropes are much weaker when wet or frozen (approximately 30% weaker according to one source), and are easier to cut when under tension.

Slings

Slings are very versatile tools. They can be used to tie various knots used in rescues, including the Mariner knot, Klemheist knot, Autoblock knot and Bachman knot, as well as a chest harness or aiders.

When tying knots using slings, I prefer to use a sewn 24-inch long section of nylon webbing that is ⁹⁄₁₆-inch wide.

Slings made of Spectra (a relatively new high-tech fiber), although very strong, do not provide adequate resistance for friction knots due to the material's slick surface.

Slings should not be used in situations where they will be exposed to excessive heat or friction. If a sling has already been exposed to these conditions, retire the sling because its reliability has been compromised.

If you need to extend the distance between two carabiners, and you are out of slings to use for this purpose, wired nuts can be used. Other pieces of gear on your rack also may have slings on them that could be used in the same way.

KNOWLEDGE

The most important tool in every rescue is your brain. Carefully survey the scene to prevent further difficulties and ensure safety. Plan your course of action carefully and, if necessary, locate assistance.

Systems

The ability to construct solid anchors and position belays correctly is required before attempting any of the skills presented in this book.

Anchors and belays are briefly described in this book. For further information, read *How to Rock Climb!* or *Climbing Anchors* by John Long.

Anchors

Each technique described in this book is based on the assumption that the anchor is *completely* reliable.

When constructing anchors it is always important to be **ERNEST.** This acronym (and the following description) is from the American Mountain Guides Association Mountain Bulletin (1996).

E- Equalized - All components in a belay anchor should be connected so any loads are distributed as evenly as possible.

To create a loop to equalize the forces on anchors, follow the steps illustrated below.

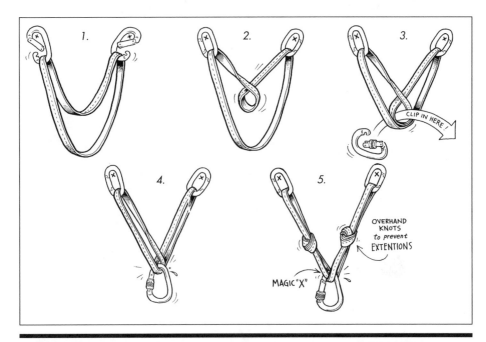

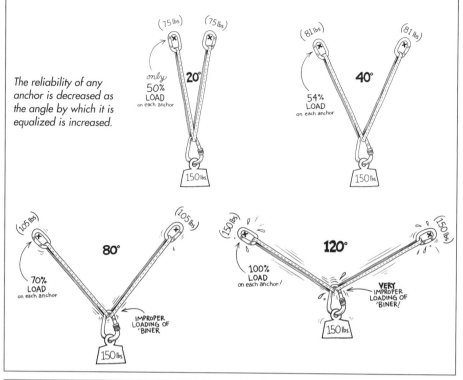

The reliability of any anchor is decreased as the angle by which it is equalized is increased.

The following statistics, compiled from the 1992 AMGA Guides Manual, show the load distribution on each of the two anchors with the slings at various angles:

- 20° = 50%
- 40° = 54%
- 80° = 70%
- 120° = 100%
- 160° = 290%

R- **Redundant** - The belay should consist of a multitude of anchor points with a minimum of two completely trustworthy pieces.

NE - **No Extensions** - The ideal belay should be constructed so that no failure by any piece(s) will cause a shock load to the system: use of a cordelette is a simple way to accomplish this.

S - **Solid** - Solid and stable means that each individual piece should be seated in as stable position as possible, loaded in the direction that it is the strongest and that the entire belay should be solid and stable regardless of the direction loaded. Remember, every belay is a potential rescue anchor and should be built to hold an upward as well as downward load.

T - **Timely** - The choice of where and when the belay should be made to maximize efficiency, safety, and communication; in general, keep your partner in sight, and avoid long wandering pitches, especially on windy days. Frequently it is safer and faster to do a climb in shorter pitches

When equalizing two anchor points, the loaded slings should ideally form an angle of 45° or less. Loading slings from 45° to 90° will decrease the effectiveness of the equalization because the load is distributed less efficiently.

Slings equalized at angles greater than 120° actually multiply the force on each individual anchor rather than decreasing that force by distributing the load. Never use slings loaded at this or any wider angle.

Carabiners with opposite and opposing gates.

Use locking carabiners or two carabiners with opposite and opposing gates to attach loads to the anchors. Use additional slings of the appropriate length, or a cordelette, to prevent shock-loading the system if one piece of the anchor fails. To prevent excessive leverage, tie-off protruding pitons with a slip knot. Older bolts – and even some new ones – may be unreliable. Back them up whenever possible.

Belays

Once you have equalized your belay anchors, create a central "power point" using two opposite/opposed carabiners, or one locking and one standard carabiner with an opposing gate. The central loop in a cordelette also can be used as the power point. However, while the cordelette offers a system that is redundant and will not shock-load the system if one piece fails, it does not truly equalize the anchors.

Attach this "power point" directly to your belay carabiner, or clip in with directional slings. Position the belay so the anchor will hold the full weight of the climber while using the belay device, sparing strain on the belayer's back. A better belay method re-directs the belay through the anchors. This method allows for quicker transitions on multi-pitch routes, reasonably comfortable hanging belays, and will simplify the steps involved in a self-rescue. When the belay is positioned correctly, it will allow the belayer to escape easily from the belay.

The re-directed belay allows the rescuer to escape the belay with greater ease and efficiency.

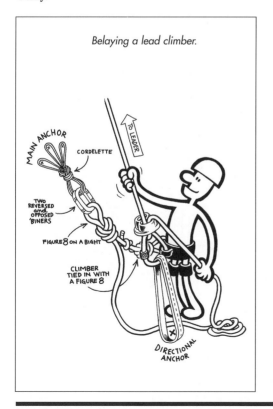

Belaying a lead climber.

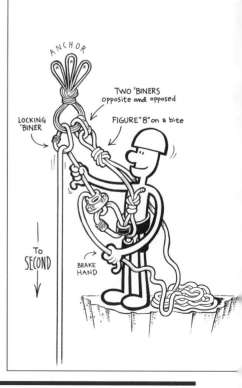

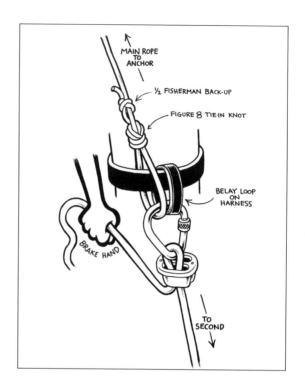

MAIN ROPE
TO
ANCHOR

½ FISHERMAN BACK-UP

FIGURE 8 TIE-IN KNOT

BELAY LOOP
ON
HARNESS

BRAKE HAND

TO
SECOND

Although an appropriate method, belaying from your waist will increase the complexity of the belay escape.

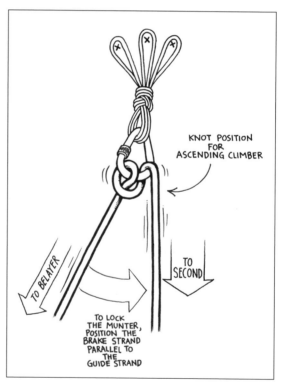

KNOT POSITION
FOR
ASCENDING CLIMBER

TO BELAYER

TO
SECOND

TO LOCK
THE MUNTER,
POSITION THE
BRAKE STRAND
PARALLEL TO
THE
GUIDE STRAND

This illustration demonstrates a belay system rigged with the Munter hitch technique.

Knots

Knots used for self-rescue include tie-in knots, friction knots, knots useful for belays, knots used to transfer loads, and a few miscellaneous knots used in other aspects of climbing or self-rescue. The ability to tie these knots and use them properly is essential for self-rescue.

TIE-IN KNOTS

Figure Eight Follow-through

This is the standard tie-in knot.

Figure Eight Follow-through.

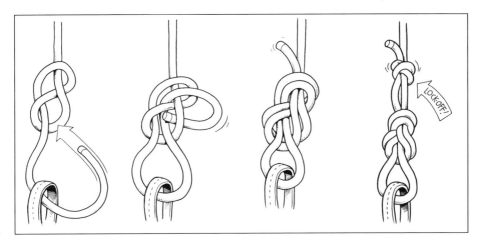

Figure Eight on a bight

The Figure Eight loop is formed using a bight of rope. This is a useful knot for backing up self-rescue systems.

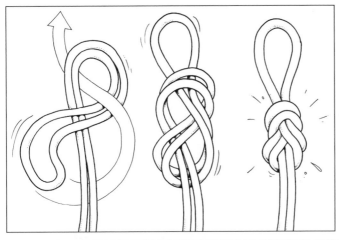

Figure Eight on a bight.

Double Bowline

This is an alternative to the Figure Eight knot.

This knot has the advantage of being easier to adjust while anchoring and easier to untie after it has been weighted.

However, three disadvantages exist. First, this knot is sometimes tied incorrectly and is more difficult to inspect visually than a Figure Eight. Second, this knot is considered "weaker" than a Figure Eight Follow-through – weaker in that there is a greater reduction in rope strength due to the bends in the knot. Third, if only tied to step number three, this knot can be untied while under a load by pulling on the strand of rope that loops around the main rope.

Double bowline.

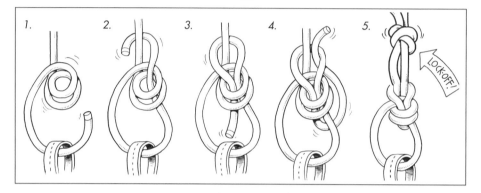

FRICTION KNOTS

Although all knots rely on friction to hold, the term "friction knot" describes knots that are used for ascending, locking, or holding a rope. Most friction knots may be formed with accessory cord or ⁹⁄₁₆-inch webbing.

The Prusik knot is used in most of the self-rescue skills described in this book. The Prusik knot can be substituted with other knots listed in the friction knot section.

Prusik

This is the classic friction knot. The standard accessory cord diameter used for this knot is six or seven millimeter. I use

Prusik knot.

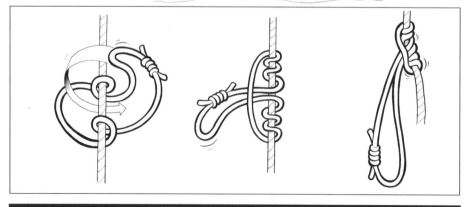

three- and four-foot lengths of cord tied into a loop with a Double Fisherman's knot (described in the miscellaneous knots section). Webbing should not be used to form a Prusik.

Klemheist

A good knot for ascending or holding, this knot is more versatile than the Prusik because it can be tied with accessory cord or %6-inch webbing.

Autoblock

Like the Klemheist knot, this is a good knot for ascending or holding. It can be tied with accessory cord or %6-inch webbing, and has the added benefit of being relatively easy to release while under a load.

Bachman

This knot is tied in conjunction with a carabiner and can be formed with accessory cord or webbing. The carabiner creates a handle for easier gripping and also helps to unlock the knot while ascending. However, if you pull down on the carabiner while ascending, you will unlock the knot. It is important that the load is placed on the protruding loop of webbing or cord under the carabiner, versus on the carabiner itself.

When constructed properly, this is one of the best knots for ascending a rope. If the rope is icy, however, the Bachman may not work. While the carabiner allows easier unlocking and is easier to grip, it decreases the friction and ability of the knot to lock against the rope.

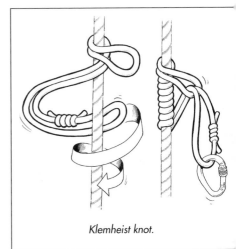

Klemheist knot.

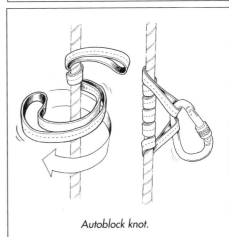

Autoblock knot.

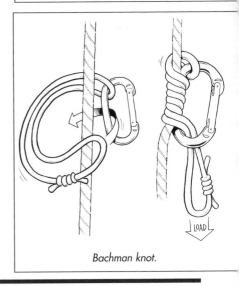

Bachman knot.

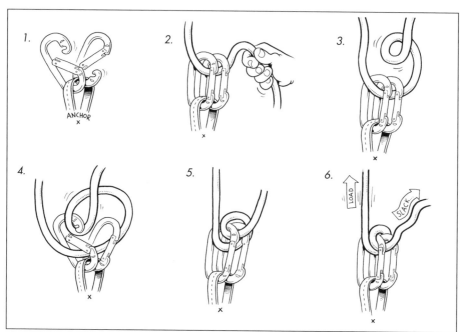

Garda Hitch.

GARDA HITCH (AKA ALPINE CLUTCH)

This hitch is formed using two identical oval carabiners. Position the carabiners so the gates open in different directions, but are next to each other. The gates must be on the same side, because the knot rides down the carabiner's smooth spine.

The Garda Hitch locks the rope so that it can move only in one direction. To free the hitch, pull on the slack rope and wedge a carabiner or nut tool between the two carabiners to unload the hitch. Then, you can transfer the load elsewhere.

KNOTS USED TO TRANSFER LOADS

In this book, the Mariner knot, Mule knot and Munter Mule combination are used to transfer loads because they can be untied while loaded. Remember to always backup and double-check the system before untying – or relying solely on – these knots!

Note: If you have loaded a knot that cannot be untied while under tension (i.e. a Figure Eight), and you need to untie the knot, construct a Z-pulley system to release and transfer the load. The Z-pulley system is described in Chapter 10/Pulley Systems.

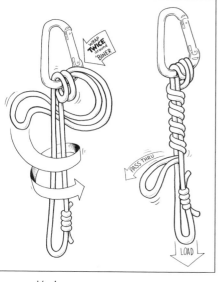

Mariner.

Mariner

Despite its intimidating appearance, this is a good knot to transfer a load. Use it to attach *one carabiner to another carabiner or sling* using accessory cord or ⅝-inch nylon webbing (not Spectra).

As a rule, the Mariner knot must be kept under tension to prevent it from accidentally untying. This knot often slips a little. Backup the Mariner knot by clipping a quickdraw from the protruding loop to the anchor. Allow enough slack in the quickdraw to prevent it from being loaded if the Mariner knot slips.

Girth hitch two lengths of webbing or cord together when you need to tie a Mariner knot and friction knot in the same sling. (The Girth Hitch is described in the miscellaneous knots section.) This allows enough length for both knots to be tied correctly.

Mule Knot with an Overhand backup

This good knot holds a load when used in conjunction with either a Munter Hitch or a belay plate. It is also a great knot to free your hands safely while belaying.

The overhand backup is necessary to prevent the Mule knot from untying. If the Mule knot alone is used to stop a rappel, it can untie itself; the weight of the rope hanging beneath the knot can apply enough pressure to untie the knot.

Note: Although the Mule knot can be untied while loaded, it can be very difficult to do so. Assume you are using a belay device and locking carabiner. If you load the Mule

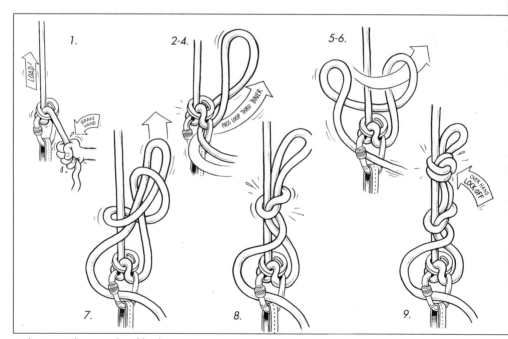

Mule Knot with an overhand backup.

knot and forget to pass the rope through the locking carabiner before tying the Mule knot, it will lock. To unlock the Mule knot, loop the free end of the rope around your foot. Stand in the loop to apply pressure to unlock the knot.

To form a Mule knot in conjunction with a belay device:

1. From the belayer's perspective, lock the belay device with your brake hand (for this example, assume the brake hand is your right hand).
2. Loop the slack (behind your brake hand) through the locking carabiner on your harness from right to left.
3. Feed the slack *under* and back to the right of the loaded rope.
4. Form a loop (half-twist – clockwise).
5. Take another bight of the slack and feed it *under* and to the left of the loaded rope.
6. Form a loop in this bight of rope (half twist – counterclockwise).
7. Feed this second loop (the left loop) *over* the loaded rope and through the first loop.
8. Tighten the knot formed with the two loops, leaving a tail.
9. Using the tail, tie an overhand knot on the loaded rope.

It is important to remember that the first loop is always taking the load and the *second* loop goes through the first (fed over the loaded rope).

Munter Mule combination

This combination can be used to tie off a loaded rope. It can also be used in place of a Mariner knot when using a cordelette.

When using the Munter Mule combination, load the Munter Hitch to correctly position the knot before you tie the Mule knot. Tie the Mule knot in front of the Munter Hitch (toward the victim and away from the belayer). Furthermore, when using the Munter Mule combination, do not pass the rope through the locking carabiner before tying the Mule knot.

Munter Mule combination.

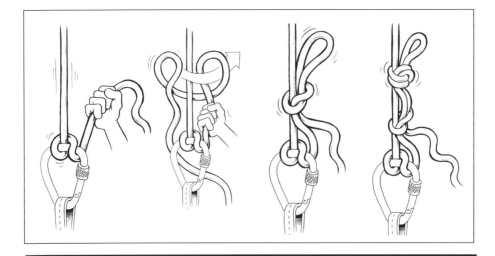

MISCELLANEOUS KNOTS

Clove Hitch

This is an easily adjusted hitch that can be used to equalize anchors or tie off pitons to reduce excess leverage. The Clove Hitch also can be used when aid soloing.

Butterfly Knot

Commonly used as a tie-in point for the middle man in a party of three during glacier travel. This knot may be used to isolate a section of rope that has been damaged.

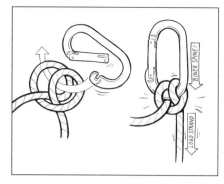

Clove Hitch.

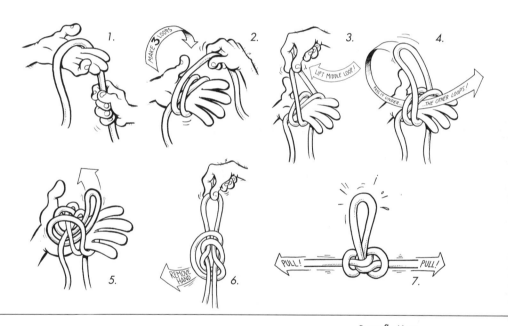

Butterfly Knot.

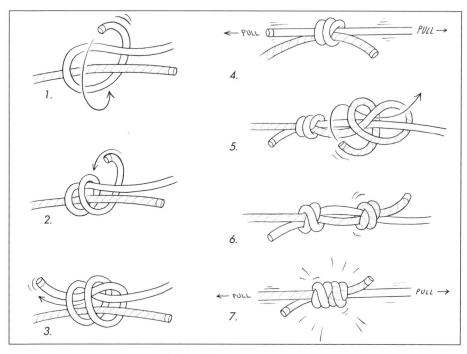

Double Fisherman's Knot.

Double Fisherman's Knot

Used to join two ropes or accessory cord together.

In-Line Figure Eight

This knot may be used when anchoring a rope, or lowering a victim and another rescuer together.

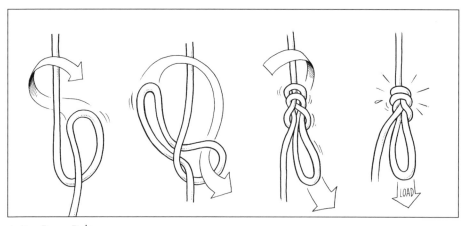

In-Line Figure Eight.

Figure Eight with a Double Fisherman's backup

Used to join two ropes together. The combination of the Figure Eight and Double Fisherman's is easier to untie than the Double Fisherman's alone.

Slip Knot

Use a slip knot to reduce excessive leverage that could break or remove a piton.

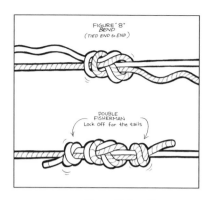

Figure Eight with a
Double Fisherman's knot
as backup.

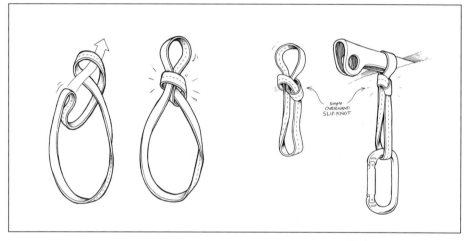

Slip knot.

Girth Hitch

Commonly used to join lengths of webbing. Throughout the rescue scenarios described in this book, the Girth Hitch is used to connect a length of webbing to a harness.

Girth Hitch.

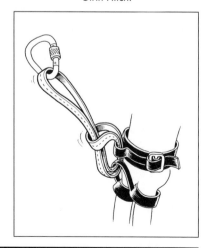

Munter Hitch

Used as a belay hitch, for rappelling, or to hold a load in conjunction with a Mule knot with an overhand knot. Use a locking, pear-style carabiner with the weighted segment of the knot toward the spine (opposite the gate) of the carabiner to preserve carabiner strength.

Munter Hitch.

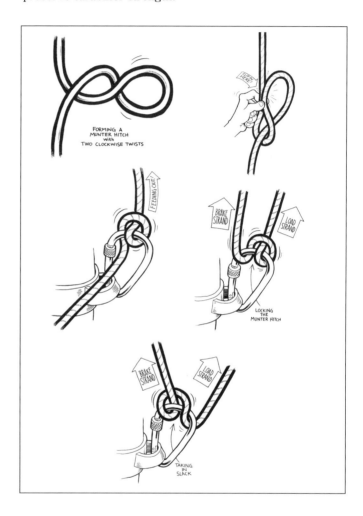

South Early Winter Spire, (5.10+), Washington Cascades.

Photo: Jim Dockery

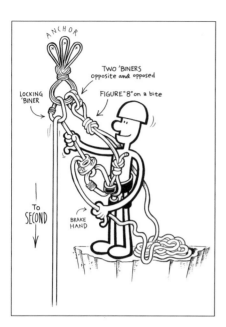

Freeing hands from a loaded belay.

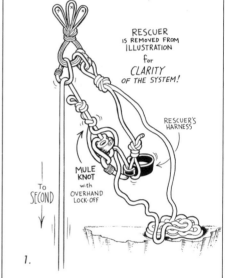

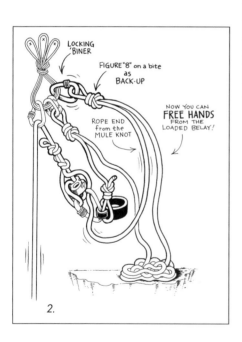

Escaping the Belay

CHAPTER 4

This chapter describes one of the most important aspects of self-rescue – how to escape a belay. This is often the first step in a successful rescue, as the rescuer needs to have his or her hands free to begin any of the techniques described in later chapters on rescuing a lead climber or a second. In addition, to escape a belay, the rescuer must use some of the most important skills in self-rescue – transferring a load using the appropriate knots and backing up a system.

This chapter consists of three parts. Parts 1 and 2 utilize a re-directed belay to free your hands and escape from the belay. Part 3 is illustrated using a waist belay.

PART 1:
FREEING HANDS FROM A LOADED BELAY

Scenario: You are belaying a climber who has weighted the rope, and you wish to take your hands off the rope. In this scenario you will be using a re-directed belay. Once you have built your anchors at about shoulder height, clip in. Next, redirect the load from your second by clipping the segment of rope used for belaying through the anchor.

1. Tie a Mule knot with an overhand backup and load the knot.
2. Using the slack, tie a Figure Eight loop and secure it to your anchors to backup the system.
3. Survey the scene. Once you have double-checked the system, you may release your hands from the rope.

To release the Mule knot:
- Unclip and untie the backup Figure Eight loop.
- Untie the Overhand knot and Mule knot.While untying the Mule knot, keep your brake hand on the rope ready to hold the load. Due to the position of the Mule knot, your brake hand is now on the opposite side of the belay carabiner.
- The load is placed back on the belay device once the knot is pulled free. Just before the knot releases, it will become tight. As you pull with the brake hand, it will "pop" free.

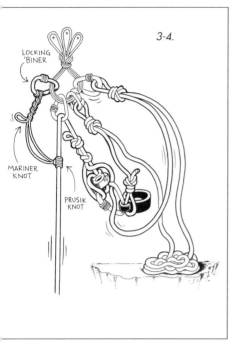

3-4.

LOCKING 'BINER

MARINER KNOT

PRUSIK KNOT

Escaping a loaded belay.

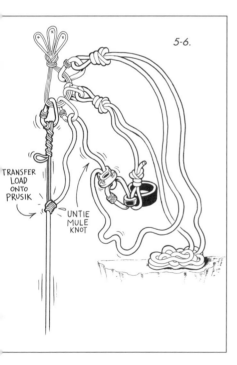

5-6.

TRANSFER LOAD ONTO PRUSIK

UNTIE MULE KNOT

PART 2:
ESCAPING A LOADED BELAY

Scenario: You are holding a climber who has weighted the rope. Your objective is to tie-off the climber/weighted rope and unclip from the belay device.

Two similar methods are described below.

Method 1: Loading the rope to the anchor with a Prusik knot

1. Tie a Mule knot with an overhand backup and load the knot.
2. Using the slack, tie a Figure Eight loop and secure it to your anchors to backup the system.
3. Tie a Prusik knot to the loaded section of the rope.
4. Attach the Prusik knot to your anchor using a Mariner knot or Munter Mule knot. If you are unable to use extra rope or a cordelette, you can extend webbing to tie the Mariner knot by:
- Girth Hitch a loop of webbing or accessory cord to the Prusik knot.
- Clip a carabiner to the anchors.
- Attaching the Girth-hitched webbing or accessory cord to the carabiner with a Mariner knot.
- To backup the Mariner knot, clip a quickdraw from the protruding loop of the Mariner knot to the anchor. Allow enough slack to prevent loading the quickdraw if the Mariner knot slips.
5. Untie the Mule knot and transfer the load to the Mariner knot and Prusik knot.
6. Survey the scene. Make sure the Prusik and Mariner knots are holding and not slipping.
7. Unclip your harness from the original belay carabiner. Next, to reduce extensions in the system, tie a Munter Mule knot to the anchor just above the loaded Prusik knot.

To load the belay back to the belay device:

1. Clip your harness back into the system with your original locking belay carabiner. Remove the Munter Mule that was tied to reduce the extension in the system. Next, tie a Mule Knot with an overhand to lock your belay device.
2. Untie and unload the Mariner knot. This will load the Mule knot.
3. Remove the Prusik knot.
4. Remove the backup Figure Eight knot attached to the anchors.
5. Untie and unload the Mule knot. This will place the load on your belay device.

Method 2: Loading the rope to the anchor with a Munter Mule combination

If the belay escape system is holding a heavy load, or has to be in place for a long period of time, this method is better than Method 1 because the load is placed on the main rope rather than on a single friction knot.

Follow steps 1 through 7 in Method 1: At this point, the load is on the Prusik and Mariner knots.

8. Release the Mariner knot and load the Munter Mule combination.
9. Retie the Mariner knot to the carabiner. Load the Mariner knot by sliding the Prusik knot down the rope.

To load the belay back to the belay device:

1. Untie and unload the Munter Mule combination to load your Prusik and Mariner knot.
2. Clip your belay carabiner to your harness. Next, attach your belay device to the rope and tie a Mule knot with an overhand.
3. Untie and unload the Mariner knot. This will load the belay device and Mule knot.
4. Remove the Prusik knot.
5. Remove the backup Figure Eight knot attached to the anchors.
6. Untie and unload the Mule knot to transfer the load back to your belay device.

Note: If you are using the Munter Mule combination, you can make a simple transition by reëstablishing the belay with a Munter Hitch.

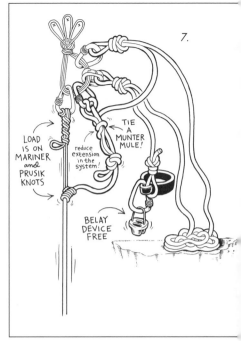

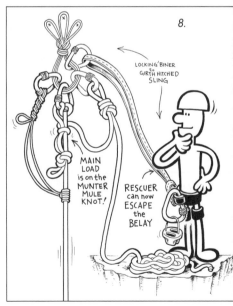

Escaping the belay using a Munter Mule combination.

PART 3:
ESCAPING FROM A LOADED BELAY

Scenario: You are belaying at the top of a pitch, and due to unforeseen circumstances, your objective is to tie-off the climber on the weighted rope and unclip from the belay device. This method utilizes the rope more than the previous methods, and assumes you are belaying off your waist. For this particular method, you must have 20 to 25 feet of slack available. Slack is provided when a pitch is less than a full rope's length, and/or when a distance of the pitch has been ascended by the second. If slack is not available, use either of the first two methods previously described to transfer the load from your belay device to the anchor. The illustrations depict a typical belay anchor.

1. Tie a Mule knot with an overhand backup and load the knot.
2. Using the slack, tie a Figure Eight loop and secure it to your anchors to backup the system.
3. Using a sling, tie a Klemheist knot to the loaded section of the rope. A Prusik knot can be used, but a Klemheist is recommended if you do not have a Prusik cord.

   Note: In this scenario, the leader has used the main rope to tie a Figure Eight on a bight and clipped it into the anchor. The other strand of rope, coming from the Figure Eight on a bight, should be slack. If there is not 20 to 25 feet of slack available, use either of the two methods described in Part 2.

4. Use the slack from the Figure Eight anchor to attach the Klemheist to the anchor. You will be loading the Figure Eight anchor, not the backup Figure Eight. To do this:
   - Clip a locking carabiner or two opposite/opposed carabiners to the Klemheist.
   - Using the slack from the Figure Eight anchor, tie a Munter Mule knot. While tying the Munter Mule knot, keep the rope very taut to the anchor.
5. Unload the Mule knot that is locking your belay device to load the Klemheist and Munter Mule knots.
6. Attach the main rope to the anchor using a Munter Mule knot. The Munter Mule knot should be kept very taut. At this point, you may need to adjust the backup Figure Eight knot.
7. You should now be free to maneuver.

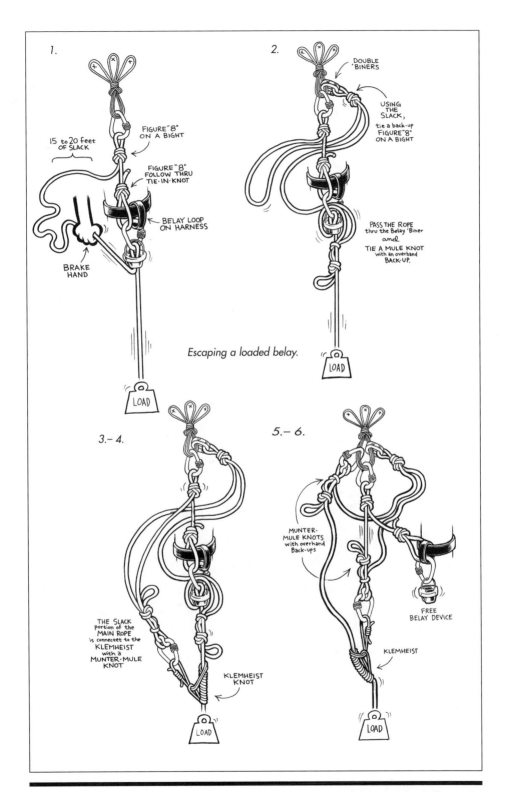

1.

FIGURE "8" ON A BIGHT

15 to 20 feet OF SLACK

FIGURE "8" FOLLOW THRU TIE·IN·KNOT

BELAY LOOP ON HARNESS

BRAKE HAND

LOAD

Escaping a loaded belay.

2.

DOUBLE 'BINERS

USING THE SLACK, tie a back-up FIGURE "8" ON A BIGHT

PASS THE ROPE thru the Belay 'Biner *and* TIE A MULE KNOT with an overhand BACK·UP.

LOAD

3.- 4.

THE SLACK portion of the MAIN ROPE is connectet to the KLEMHEIST with a MUNTER·MULE KNOT

KLEMHEIST KNOT

LOAD

5.- 6.

MUNTER· MULE KNOTS with overhand Back-ups

FREE BELAY DEVICE

KLEMHEIST

LOAD

*Rappelling necessitates
specific techniques for
self-rescue.*

Jim Dockery photo

Rappelling and Ascending

Getting up and down a fixed rope quickly and safely is an integral part of climbing. These skills are necessary for preventing as well as executing a self-rescue. Also discussed in this chapter are ways to escape a self-belay device, ascender or loaded friction knot.

DESCENDING A ROPE

The art of rappelling is not a mystery to most climbers. However, many climbers could use a few additional techniques to guarantee safety and provide for unusual circumstances. Whether you are involved in a rescue, or simply descending from a pleasure climb, always backup your rappel.

Backup for a Rappel

The traditional method of backing up a rappel consisted of tying a Prusik knot above your rappel device and attaching it to your harness. However, if you load the Prusik knot while rappelling it is very difficult to release.

The newer method utilizes an Autoblock knot positioned below the rappel device and attached to a leg loop on your harness. To prevent jamming, the length of this backup system must be shorter than the distance from your leg loop to your rappel device. A good way to do this is to extend your rappel device above your harness with either a doubled or Girth Hitched sling prior to rappelling.

As you rappel, hold the top of the knot with your brake hand. This will allow the Autoblock to slide over the rope. If you remove your brake hand, the Autoblock will hold the rope in the brake position. Since the Autoblock simply replaces the brake hand if the rapeller lets go, it takes less force to keep the rappel device locked. Therefore, this knot is easily unloaded by applying downward pressure to the top of the knot after it has been weighted. There are a couple of ways to construct this system.

Although the traditional method to back-up a rappel will work, it can be very difficult to release.

1. This version allows you to pre-rig the Autoblock backup. Simply take a twenty-inch loop of four-to five-mm accessory cord and Girth Hitch it to your leg loop on the braking side of your harness. Loop the remaining cord around your leg loop and tie it off so it will not get in the way while climbing. When you need to use the Autoblock backup, unravel the cord from your leg loop, keeping the Girth Hitch in

PRUSIK clipped into the HARNESS

place. Wrap the cord around the rope about four times - toward your belay device - to form the Autoblock. Complete the Autoblock by clipping the remaining loop to your leg loop with a carabiner.

2. If you do not have a twenty-inch loop, and you need to improvise, this method also works. Girth Hitch a short section of cord or webbing to your leg loop. Next, tie an Autoblock knot on the rappel rope and attach it to the cord or webbing on the leg loop with a carabiner.

Warning! Always tie a knot in the end(s) of the rope before rappelling! Experienced climbers have been killed by rappelling off the end of a rope.

Note: If you tied your Autoblock incorrectly and you are unable to unlock it, simply loop a section of rope around your foot and stand to un-weight and unlock the Autoblock.

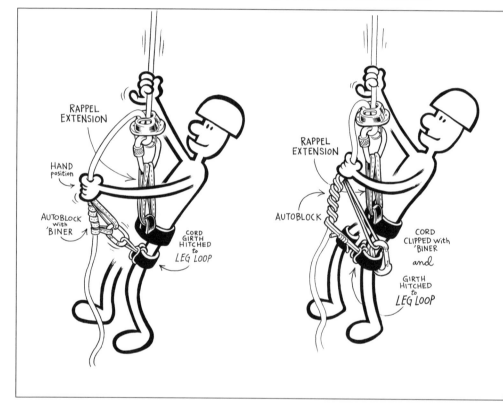

These are two examples of autoblock backup for a rappel.

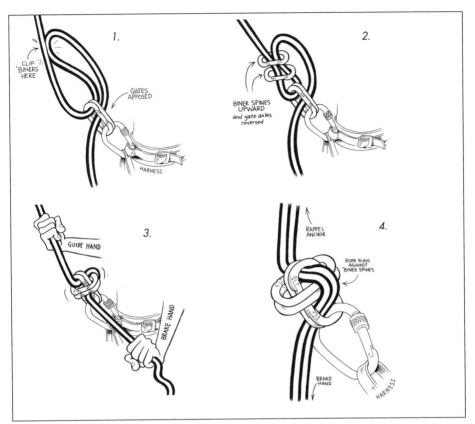

Construction of a carabiner brake.

Alternative Rappel Devices

Two alternatives to modern rappel/belay devices include the classic carabiner brake and Munter Hitch.

The carabiner brake rappel requires four to six similar oval or D carabiners. In setting up this rappel, make sure the gates of the braking carabiners are reversed—but not reversed and opposed—as the rope will run over this pair.

If you do not have a rappel device—or the carabiners and memory to form a carabiner brake—use a Munter Hitch on a locking pear-style carabiner. When tying the Munter Hitch, the loaded segment of the rope should be positioned toward the spine of the carabiner (opposite the gate) to preserve carabiner strength.

Munter Hitch rappel.

STOPPING A DESCENT

The Autoblock backup is the preferred method to stop a descent and free your hands while rappelling. However, depending on your circumstances, there are other ways to stop a descent and free your hands that may be useful.

1. Wrap the slack rope around your upper thigh three times and let the remaining slack hang free. To backup, loop the rope under your butt and tie a Figure Eight loop. Clip the loop to the front of your harness, on the opposite side from the brake/thigh wrap.

2. The Fireman's Belay – Have someone weight the free end of the rope from the bottom of the rappel. This method is helpful when instructing beginners, cleaning a pitch on rappel (especially with "welded" RP nuts), or assisting a climber who is descending with a heavy pack.

Other methods used to stop a descent include:

1. Leg wrap

2. Fireman's belay

Retrieving a Rappel Rope

It is very important for the first person rappelling to make sure the rope can be retrieved once the rappel is completed. To do this, from the bottom of the rappel, simply pull one end of the rope down for approximately one meter. If the rope will not slide through the anchor, the climber remaining at the anchor must reposition the rappel rope or extend the anchor with slings.

ASCENDING A ROPE

The standard method of ascending a rope is to use two mechanical ascenders or two friction knots. Once you feel confident ascending with mechanical ascenders or two friction knots, try ascending a rope using a single friction knot. When practicing, use a separate rope and belayer to ensure safety. Do a least one free-hanging ascent, in which the rope is not touching the rock for a large portion of the ascent.

Although this manual focuses on techniques requiring minimal equipment, *never* attempt to "Batman" (pull yourself hand over hand) up a rope. You will be setting yourself up for a long fall and a nasty rope burn.

Ascending with Mechanical Ascenders

1. Attach two mechanical ascenders to the fixed rope.
2. Attach an aider to each ascender. An aider or etrier is basically a step ladder made of nylon.
3. Girth Hitch two daisy chains or slings to your harness. A daisy chain is a section of webbing containing loops used to adjust the distance to the clip-in point.
4. Clip each daisy chain or sling to its own ascender with a locking carabiner. The top daisy chain or sling should be of a length that allows it to comfortably hold your weight after sliding the upper ascender up the rope.

   Note: Using slings of the appropriate length may eliminate a potential point of failure (i.e. a carabiner becoming unclipped). To avoid this, Girth Hitch the sling to the ascender. Next, Girth Hitch the system to your harness.

5. Attach four carabiners or two locking carabiners to your harness.
6. To backup, tie a Figure Eight loop below your ascenders. Attach the loop to your harness with two opposite/opposing carabiners or a locking carabiner.
7. Step into the aider of the lower ascender and stand while sliding the upper ascender up the rope.
8. Transfer your weight to the highest ascender by sitting down slightly. Your harness and the upper ascender will hold your weight, enabling a short rest. Slide the lower ascender up the rope.
9. Repeat steps 7 and 8 to ascend.
10. Regularly backup the system. Every 15 feet (depending

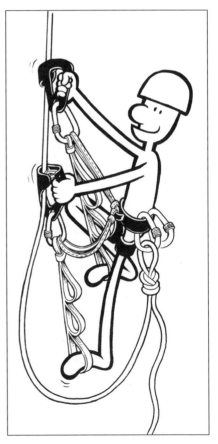

Using mechanical ascenders.

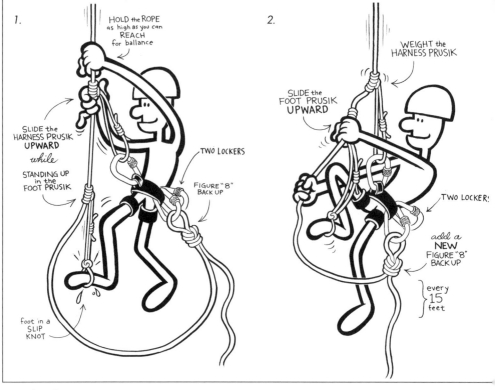

1. HOLD the ROPE as high as you can REACH for ballance

SLIDE the HARNESS PRUSIK UPWARD *while* STANDING UP in the FOOT PRUSIK

TWO LOCKERS

FIGURE "8" BACK UP

foot in a SLIP KNOT

2. WEIGHT the HARNESS PRUSIK

SLIDE the FOOT PRUSIK UPWARD

TWO LOCKER!

add a NEW FIGURE "8" BACK UP

every 15' feet

Ascending the rope using two Prusik knots.

on speed and safety margins), tie a Figure Eight loop and attach it to your harness. Once clipped into the new loop, unclip and untie the previous Figure Eight loop.

Note: Some climbers prefer to keep all of their backup knots clipped into their harness, instead of untying and releasing the previous knot. This reduces the likelihood of the rope snagging far beneath you while you are ascending. The loops of rope, however, become cumbersome while ascending.

Warning! If you use mechanical ascender and are climbing sideways (perhaps while cleaning or ascending a traverse), be aware that the rope can – and does – twist out of the ascenders. A carabiner clipped from the lower portion of the ascender to the rope you are climbing will help keep the ascender in its proper position, preventing it from torquing off the rope. Consult the directions that came with your particular ascenders for specific information.

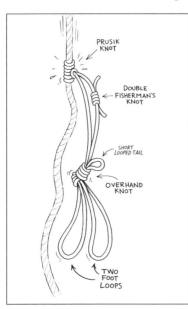

PRUSIK KNOT

DOUBLE FISHERMAN'S KNOT

SHORT LOOPED TAIL

OVERHAND KNOT

TWO FOOT LOOPS

A cordelette used to construct two foot loops.

Ascending with a Single Friction Knot

1. Attach a friction knot to the fixed rope. I prefer the Bachman knot because it is easier to unload and has a carabiner handle that is easier to grip. However, don't use a Bachman if the rope is icy.
2. Attach the Bachman knot to your harness using a locking carabiner or two opposite/opposing carabiners.
   - Optional – Girth Hitch a quickdraw to your harness and attach it to the rope with a carabiner. This helps to keep you close to the rope, making the ascent more efficient and easier.
3. Backup with a Figure Eight loop tied under the friction knot and attached to your harness with two opposite/opposing carabiners or a locking carabiner. Leave enough slack to form a foot loop.
4. There are many variations to the following method of actually ascending the rope. This version is described because it requires minimal equipment:
   a. Lift your right foot high as if making a step.
   b. Take a loop of slack from the rope hanging under the friction knot with your right hand and loop the rope beneath your right foot.
   c. Hold the slack end of the rope and the fixed rope together in your right hand.
   d. Step down with your right foot into the loop of rope as if it were an aider. With your left hand, slide the friction knot up the rope as you stand.
   e. When you have slid the Bachman knot as high as you can, weight it by sitting down slightly.
   f. Adjust the loop on your foot by pulling upward on the slack end of the rope while high-stepping.
   g. Repeat steps c through f to ascend.
   h. Regularly backup the system. Every 15 feet (depending on speed and safety margins) tie a Figure Eight loop and attach it to your harness. Once clipped into the new knot, unclip and untie the previous Figure Eight loop.

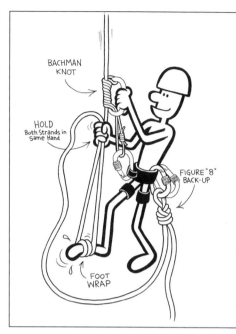

Ascending the rope with a single friction knot.

Foot Sling with a Garda Hitch

To ease the difficulty of ascending with a single friction knot, I highly recommend tying a slip knot or using a Girth Hitch in a sling and securing it to your foot. Loop the slack portion of the rope through a Garda Hitch attached to the sling. This sliding stirrup will save time and effort spent looping your foot with the slack rope.

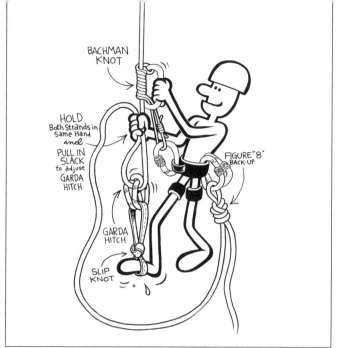

Ascending using a Garda Hitch.

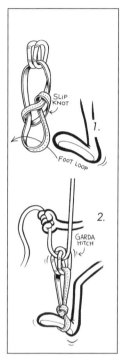

Building a foot sling using a Garda Hitch.

Notes:

For most situations, you should use two friction knots to ascend a rope—one knot for locking and ascending and the other knot as a sling for your foot.

If you have difficulty attaching the carabiners that are used to attach the backup Figure Eight knot to your harness, Girth Hitch a short sling to your harness and clip the carabiners through the quickdraw.

If you need to ascend a rope and you are weighting the end of that rope, you will need two Prusiks to ascend—one for ascending/holding, and one as a sling for your foot.

Warning! Remember, the webbing or accessory cord that you use for ascending may weaken or tear due to the friction created by rubbing against the rope. Before and after ascending with a friction knot, inspect the webbing or accessory cord for signs of wear.

ESCAPING A SELF-BELAY DEVICE, ASCENDER, OR LOADED FRICTION KNOT

Included in this section are techniques that may be used to descend a rope that you have ascended using Prusik knots or mechanical ascenders. Also included is a note describing how to escape a self-belay device. A self-belay device is a mechanical device which allows the climber to climb without a partner. These devices typically utilize a cam which will lock on a fixed rope if the climber falls. This sequence utilizes the Autoblock knot, attached below an extended rappel device, to make the transition.

Scenario - You have used Prusik knots, or ascenders, to ascend a rope. You wish to descend the rope prior to reaching an anchor. Typically, the anchor would allow you to redistribute your weight. Throughout the sequence, a Prusik knot will be described. Therefore, to escape an ascender simply substitute ascender for Prusik knot.

1. At this point, the top Prusik knot is loaded.
2. Tie a Figure Eight loop in the rope approximately four meters below the loaded Prusik knot. Clip the loop to your harness with a locking carabiner or two opposite/opposing carabiners to backup the system.
3. Below the top/loaded Prusik knot, attach a rappel device to your harness. Use a Girth Hitched, or doubled, sling to extend your rappel device off of your harness.

Note: In order to ease the transition, the extended rappel device should be approximately six inches under the loaded Prusik knot. This will prevent them from jamming due to "system stretch". However, the belay device must be extended enough so that the Autoblock does not jam. The transition can still be completed without the six inch buffer, it is simply more awkward if you are free-hanging.

4. Attach an Autoblock backup below your rappel device.
5. Firmly, take up the slack under the loaded Prusik knot and guide the rope through your rappel device.
6. Firmly, slide the Autoblock up the rope to load the belay device.
7. Unload the top Prusik knot. To do so you can either:
    a. If you have used a Prusik for your foot to ascend the rope, stand in loop. This Prusik should be positioned below the Autoblock.

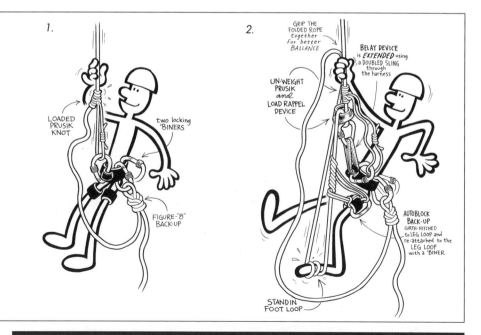

1.

LOADED
PRUSIK
KNOT

two locking
'BINERS

FIGURE-"8"
BACK-UP

2.

GRIP THE
FOLDED ROPE
together
for better
BALLANCE

UN-WEIGHT
PRUSIK
and
LOAD RAPPEL
DEVICE

BELAY DEVICE
is *EXTENDED* using
a DOUBLED SLING
through
the harness

AUTOBLOCK
BACK-UP
GIRTH-HITCHED
to LEG LOOP and
re-attached to the
LEG LOOP
with a 'BINER

STAND IN
FOOT LOOP

b. Loop the rope around your foot just as you would to ascend a rope with a single Prusik knot. Hold the free end of the rope and the fixed rope in the same hand. Stand in the loop.

8. Remove the Prusik knot. To so you can either:
   a. Loosen the Prusik knot, slide it down the rope and load the Autoblock. Next, remove the Prusik knot - this requires the six inch buffer due to "system stretch".
   b. Remove the loaded Prusik while you are standing in the lower Prusik loop or loop of rope.

9. Remove the Figure Eight backup and rappel.

Note: This system can also be used to escape a self-belay device. Assume you have weighted the device and wish to descend. Depending on your self-belay system, you can either begin from step 2; or you will need to add a Prusik knot above your self-belay device prior to beginning the sequence. This added Prusik, although more complex, may be needed to allow room for you to remove your self-belay device and extend your rappel device.

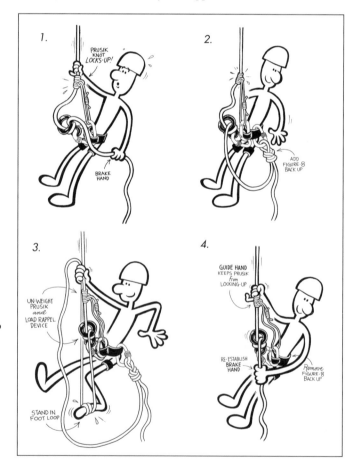

The traditional method to backup a belay frequently stranded the climber from the Prusik knot. If, due to poor choice, you have used this method the illustration sequence shown here will unlock the Prusik knot.

Passing Knots   CHAPTER   6

This chapter covers two scenarios in which a rescuer must pass a knot which is connecting two ropes. These sections describe passing a knot while lowering a victim, and passing a knot while on rappel.

PASSING A KNOT WHILE LOWERING A VICTIM

Scenario: You are lowering a climber from an anchor. You have tied two ropes together with a Double Fisherman's, or any other acceptable knot, to get the victim to the ground quickly. Because you have tied two ropes together, you need to get the knot past the belay device. Two methods are described.

The first, as well as the preferred, method utilizes two lowering points. The second lowering point is built above the first to create a simple transition when passing the knot. Ideally, this method is pre-rigged prior to lowering the victim to extend the first lowering point and tie the appropriate knots.

The second method will utilize only one lowering point. Typically, this method is more time consuming. However, depending on you circumstances, you may be unable to establish a separate lowering point above your original lowering point.

Method 1- Passing a knot using two lowering points.

Set-up:
   a. From your anchor, use slings to extend a lowering device below this point.
   b. Next, attach a locking, pear style carabiner to your anchor. Attach your second rope, used to extend the lowering process, to the pear carabiner. The second rope is attached to the pear carabiner just above the Double Fisherman's, using a Munter Mule knot.

Note: When attaching a second lowering device above the original, a Munter Hitch -versus a belay device- is used to allow the rescuer to lock the rope in place from below.

   c. Position the first rope so it is running through your lowering device.
   d. Attach a Prusik knot to the first rope, below the lowering device, and connect it to the anchor using a Mariner knot or Munter Mule on a cordelette.
1. Lower the climber using the lowering device, while moni-

toring the Prusik knot so it does not lock.

2. Approximately two feet before the Double Fisherman's reaches the lowering device, allow the Prusik knot to lock the rope in place. The closer the Double Fisherman's is to the lowering device, the easier the transition. However, if the Double Fisherman's locks in the belay device, a separate Munter Mule and Prusik combination will be needed to free the lowering device.

3. At this point the Munter Mule knot, tied above the Double Fisherman's, is the backup. However, you may decide to add a Figure Eight backup, behind the Munter Mule knot on the second rope, as an extra precaution.

4. Release your belay device from the rope. The load is now on the Mariner or Munter Mule knot.

Note: If using the Mariner knot, Girth Hitch a sling or accessory cord through the protruding loop of the Mariner knot. When the Mariner knot is released, any slack in the rope will shock-load the rope. The additional length provided by the Girth Hitched sling will allow the loaded rope to be lowered further than the original Mariner knot will allow. The extra length will be useful once you have passed the knot around the belay device - see further notes.

Passing a knot while lowering a victim via the Munter Mule method.

5. Untie the Mariner, or Munter Mule knot, to load the second rope and the Munter Mule which is tied above the Double Fisherman's.

6. Pull on the Mule knot to "pop" it free and continue to lower using the Munter Hitch.

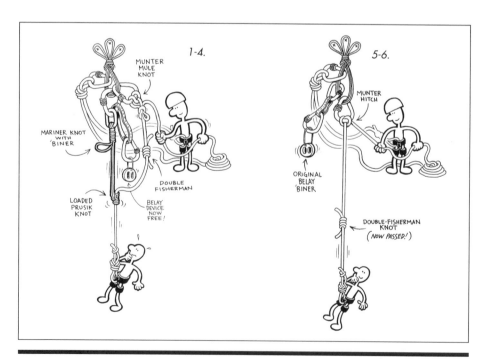

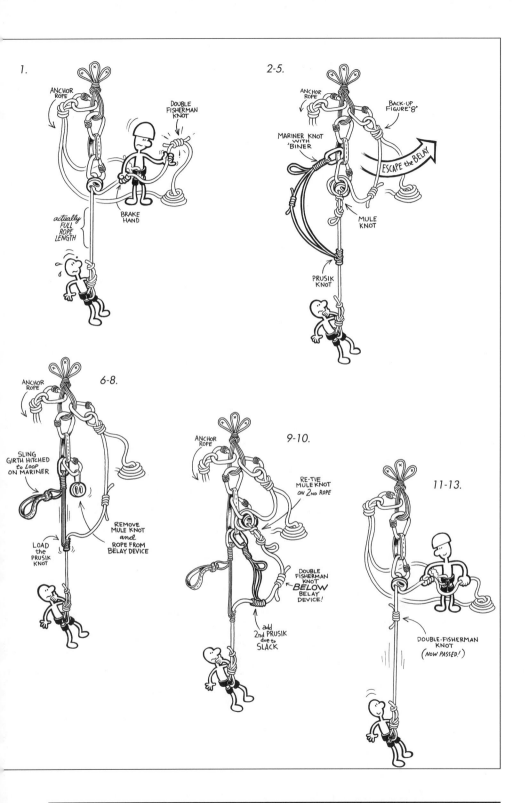

System two - Passing a knot using one lowering point.

1. You are lowering the rope through a belay device and you have not had an opportunity to pre-rig the system.
2. One meter before the knot reaches the belay device, tie a Mule knot with an overhand to stop the lower and free your hands.
3. To backup, tie a Figure Eight loop and attach it to your anchor. To allow enough rope to work with, tie the loop three meters behind the knot connecting the two ropes.
4. Attach a Prusik knot to the loaded rope. The Prusik knot is attached under the belay device and towards the victim.
5. Attach the Prusik knot to your anchors with a Mariner or Munter Mule knot.
6. Untie the Mule knot which locked the belay device, but keep your hand on the brake end of the rope.
7. Gently release slack, monitoring the Prusik knot so it does not lock, until the knot connecting the two ropes is about two feet from the belay device. The closer the knot is to the belay device, the easier the transition.
8. Lock the Prusik knot in place. Be very careful not to jam the Double Fisherman's knot in the belay device.
9. Unclip the rope from the belay device and re-clip the rope after passing the knot around the belay device.

Note: At this point you may be able to connect the second rope behind the belay device using a Munter Mule knot. If so, the remainder of the sequence is simplified and the first method, Passing a knot using two lowering points, can be used.

10. Once the knot has been passed around the belay device, position the knot connecting the ropes close to the belay device and tie a Mule knot with an overhand. Follow these steps:
    a. Attach another Prusik knot just below the knot connecting the two ropes and attach this new knot to the anchor with a Mariner or Munter Mule knot.
    b. Untie the original Mariner or Munter Mule knot to load the new Prusik knot. Remove the original Prusik knot from the rope.

Note: This transfer is generally, but not always, necessary to decrease the amount of slack in your system so you can retrieve your original Prusik knot.

11. Untie the new Mariner or Munter Mule knot to load the belay device and Mule knot which is locking the belay device.
12. Untie the Figure Eight backup.
13. Remove the Prusik knot, unload the Mule knot, and continue to lower the victim.

Notes:
Unless you are careful with your rope-handling, the Prusik knot will be out of reach after you release the Mariner knot. You will be forced to leave the Prusik on the rope. This may cause the rope to snag during the lower.

When tying the Prusik knot to the rope, the knot that makes a loop of the accessory cord (Double Fisherman's) should be close to the rope so it does not interfere with the Mariner knot.

Before you Girth Hitch cord or webbing through the protruding loop of the Mariner knot, make sure the knot is tied correctly. The Mariner knot should finish by wrapping around itself at least three times before it is threaded between the cord or webbing under tension. If not, the section to which the webbing has been Girth-hitched to extend its length will jam in the Mariner knot and be difficult to release.

Assisted Lower

This system can be used to quickly lower a victim or an inexperienced climber two full rope lengths without establishing a new rappel station or passing a knot. When utilizing this system, the rescuer cannot stay close to the victim while descending, so if the victim is injured, the rescuer should use the assisted or counter-weight rappel. Furthermore, if there are more than two pitches involved, the victim must be able to anchor to a new rappel station without assistance so that the rescuer can retrieve the rappel ropes and continue the descent.

Scenario: You are two pitches up a route, climbing with double ropes, and a lightning storm moves in. Your partner is new to climbing and you do not feel confident that he can retreat from the climb safely. Your objective is to retreat from the second pitch quickly while remaining in control of your partner's safety.

For clarity, I will refer to the two ropes as the White rope and the Black rope. The White rope is used by the victim to rappel and must be shorter than the Black rope. The Black rope is used by the rescuer to belay the victim during the rappel and lower the victim after the rappel.

1. Arrange belay anchors to allow the victim to rappel.
2. Join the two ropes.
3. The victim ties into the end of the White rope. The ropes need to be set up so that the White rope is shorter than the Black rope. This prevents loading the belay rope once the victim reaches the end of his rappel. To prevent the belay rope, or Black rope, from being improperly loaded, follow these steps:
   a. From the victim's tie-in knot, measure out approximately eight feet of slack on the White rope.

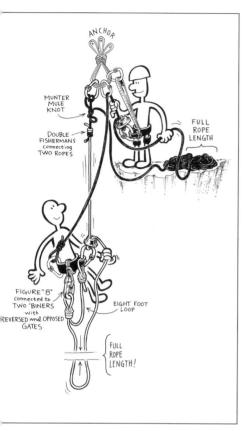

ANCHOR

MUNTER
MULE
KNOT

DOUBLE
FISHERMANS
connecting
TWO ROPES

FULL
ROPE
LENGTH

FIGURE "8"
connected to
TWO 'BINERS
with
REVERSED and OPPOSED
GATES

EIGHT FOOT
LOOP

FULL
ROPE
LENGTH!

Assisted lower.

b. Tie a Figure Eight loop and attach it to the victim's harness using two reversed and opposed carabiners.

4. The joined ropes are attached to the anchor using a Munter Mule knot tied on the Black rope. The Munter Mule is attached to the anchor just above the knot used to join the two ropes.

5. The victim sets up a rappel on the White rope, attaching the rappel device just beneath the knot used to join the ropes.

6. Attach a locking carabiner to the victim's harness and clip the other end of the Black rope to the locking carabiner.

7. The victim rappels down the White rope while the rescuer belays him using the Black rope.

8. The victim rappels to the end of the White rope. The Figure Eight loop, which is attached to the victim's harness using two carabiners, will halt the rappel.

9. The victim unclips the Black rope that was used for a backup belay.

10. The rescuer releases the Mule knot and lowers the victim using the Munter Hitch.

11. Once the victim is on the ground, he unties from the rope.

12. At this point the rescuer can either pull up the ropes and set-up a multiple rappel to the ground, or rappel down the joined ropes passing a knot en route.

Note: If the eight-foot section of rope used to shorten the White rope is needed to reach the ground, a few options are available. Probably the simplest solution is to have the victim use a backup friction knot during his rappel, such as an Autoblock attached to a leg loop. Instruct the victim to load the Autoblock knot just before the Figure Eight knot connected to the two carabiners reaches the rappel device. At that point, the victim will need to unclip from the Black rope. Next, he will unclip the White rope and continue the rappel until his tie-in knot halts the rappel.

PASSING A KNOT WHILE RAPPELLING

This section describes methods of passing a knot connecting two ropes while on either a low-angled or a free-hanging rappel. Such a scenario would be encountered when two ropes are tied together for a full rope-length counter-weight rappel – or if a particular circumstance requires passing a knot on rappel.

AUTOBLOCK METHOD

Scenario: You are rappelling down a rope and your objective is to pass a knot around the rappel device. This method is used for low-angled rappels.

1. Load an Autoblock knot connected above your rappel device. This will stop the rappel before your rappel device reaches the knot connecting the two ropes.

   Note: The Autoblock is used because it can, with practice, be released while under tension. The distance from the Autoblock knot to your harness should be just less than an arm's length.

2. To backup, clip a Figure Eight loop to your harness. The Figure Eight loop should be tied at least three meters below the knot connecting the two ropes.
3. Unclip the rappel device and re-attach it under the knot connecting the two ropes.
4. To backup the rappel,
   a. tie another Autoblock knot on the rappel rope beneath the rappel device, and attach it to the leg loop of your harness with a short section of cord or webbing, and extend your rappel device using a doubled or Girth Hitched sling.
5. Grasp the top of the first Autoblock firmly and pull downward to unload the Autoblock.
6. Once you have loosened the Autoblock, the load will be placed on your rappel device and the second Autoblock that is attached to your leg loop.

   Note: If there isn't enough slack in the system to transfer your weight to the belay device, you will need to pull yourself up the rope a short distance to release the original Autoblock knot from the rope, or, prior to beginning the rappel, you will need to use a cordelette to form a "releaseable Autoblock." To do this, clip the cordelette into a locking carabiner, wrap the cordelette around the rope to form the Autoblock, and attach the other strand of the cordelette to the locking carabiner with a Munter Mule knot. To load your belay device and Autoblock backup, release the Munter Mule, which will unravel the Autoblock.

7. Untie the Figure Eight loop, loosen the lower Autoblock and continue to rappel.

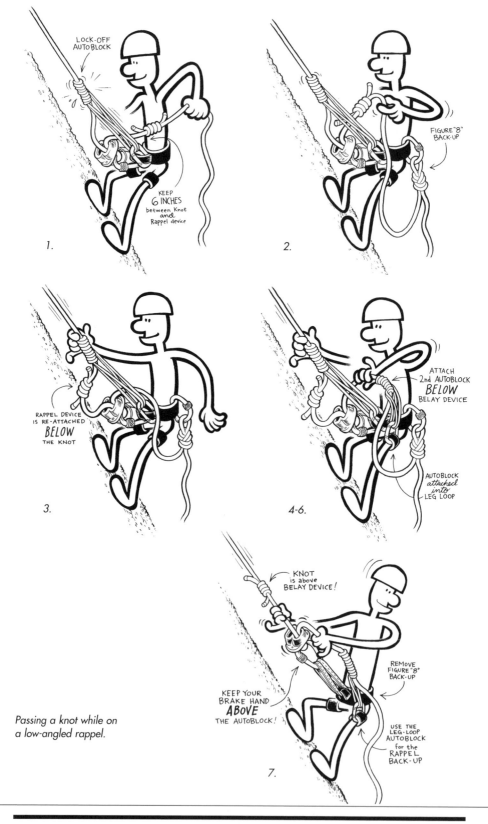

Passing a knot while on a low-angled rappel.

STEP LADDER METHOD

Scenario: Your are attempting to pass a knot, assume a Double Fisherman's knot, while on a free hanging rappel. While attempting to release your Autoblock from either its original locking position, or from its resting position on top of the Double Fisherman's, you are unable to get into position to unload the knot.

This problem arises due to the slack which has been created in the system. This slack is created from the space left between your belay device and the Double Fisherman's—the space was needed to prevent the knot from jamming in the rappel device. Slack was also created by passing your rappel device around the Double Fisherman's knot, and from extending your rappel device for the Autoblock backup.

In this sequence, you will construct a short step ladder to enable you to take your weight off the Autoblock.

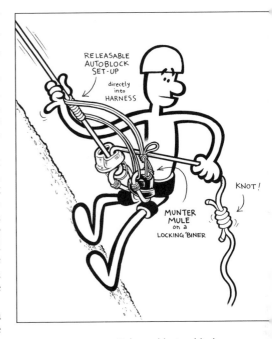

Releaseable Autoblock setup.

1. The Autoblock, used to halt your descent and pass your rappel device around the Double Fisherman's, is locked on top of the Double Fisherman's. You need to un-weight the knot to release it.
2. Prior to releasing your belay device, you should tie a Figure Eight backup knot and attach it to your harness.
3. Extend your rappel device using a Girth Hitched, or doubled, sling.
4. Attach an Autoblock backup below your rappel device.
5. Firmly, take up the slack under the Double Fisherman's knot and guide the rope through your rappel device.
6. Firmly, slide the Autoblock up the rope to load the belay device.
7. Girth Hitch two slings together and attach them to the main rope, above you rappel device and just below the Double Fisherman's using a Prusik knot.
8. Stand in the step ladder, and remove the knot resting on the Double Fisherman's.
9. Redistribute your weight onto the rappel device and the Autoblock backup.
10. Remove the Figure Eight backup and continue your rappel.

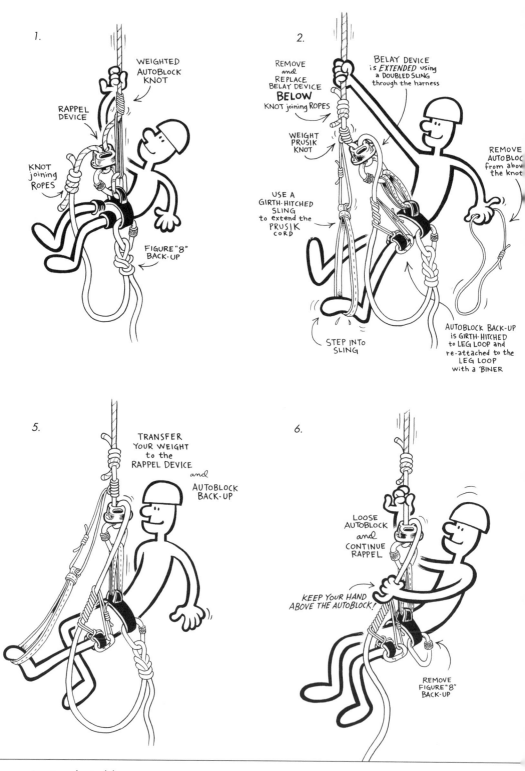

1.
WEIGHTED
AUTOBLOCK
KNOT
RAPPEL
DEVICE
KNOT
joining
ROPES
FIGURE "8"
BACK-UP

2.
REMOVE
and
REPLACE
BELAY DEVICE
BELOW
KNOT joining ROPES
BELAY DEVICE
is *EXTENDED* using
a DOUBLED SLING
through the harness
WEIGHT
PRUSIK
KNOT
REMOVE
AUTOBLOCK
from above
the knot
USE A
GIRTH-HITCHED
SLING
to extend the
PRUSIK
CORD
STEP INTO
SLING
AUTOBLOCK BACK-UP
is GIRTH-HITCHED
to LEG LOOP and
re-attached to the
LEG LOOP
with a 'BINER

5.
TRANSFER
YOUR WEIGHT
to the
RAPPEL DEVICE
and
AUTOBLOCK
BACK-UP

6.
LOOSE
AUTOBLOCK
and
CONTINUE
RAPPEL
*KEEP YOUR HAND
ABOVE THE AUTOBLOCK!*
REMOVE
FIGURE "8"
BACK-UP

*Passing a knot while on
a free-hanging rappel.*

Assisted and Counter-Weight Rappels

This chapter describes two methods of rappelling with a victim. In an assisted rappel, the rescuer and the victim descend the same rope while sharing the same rappel device. In the counter-weight rappel, the rescuer and the victim descend the same rope while counter-balancing one another.

ASSISTED RAPPEL

The assisted rappel, as described above, is a technique by which the rescuer and the victim descend the same rope, in close proximity, while sharing the *same* rappel device. This scenario would be encountered if the victim is unable to rappel without assistance due to injury or inexperience.

1. Attach a rappel device and locking carabiner through both strands of the rappel ropes. The ropes must be doubled to retrieve them after the rappel.

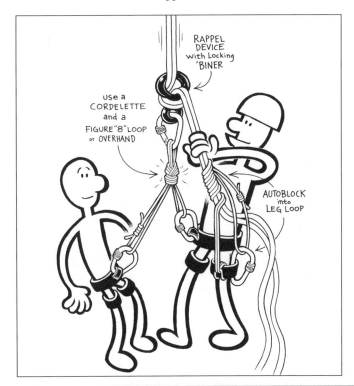

Assited rappel in the locked position.

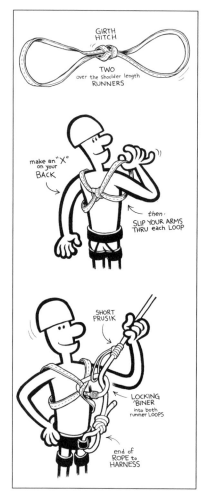

TWO
over the shoulder length
RUNNERS

make an "X"
on your
BACK

then:
SLIP YOUR ARMS
THRU each LOOP

SHORT
PRUSIK

LOCKING
'BINER
into both
runner LOOPS

end of
ROPE to
HARNESS

Construction of a chest
harness.

*Note: The rope ends should always be tied togeth-
er prior to beginning the rappel to prevent rappelling off the end of the rope.*

2. To avoid the "bumper car syndrome" attach
slings of different lengths, or a cordelette with
the Figure Eight loop tied off center, to the
locking rappel carabiner.

3 Attach each sling or loop in the cordelette to
the rescuer's and victim's harness using a
locking carabiner for each harness.

*Note: The length of the sling that the victim is
attached to may be adjusted for different circumstances. A short sling allows the victim to be sup-
ported in the rescuer's lap while descending. A
sling equal in length to that attached to the rescuer enables the victim to descend next to the rescuer. However, this can cause the "bumper car
syndrome." Generally, I prefer to use a longer
sling which allows the victim to descend beneath
the rescuer. This set-up allows the rescuer to carry
the victim piggyback, if injured, and ensures that
the rappel device is in reach. Also, the rescuer is
typically looking down to follow the easiest line of
descent and find the next suitable rappel station.*

4. To backup the rappel, tie an Autoblock knot
on the rappel rope, beneath the rappel device.
The Autoblock should be attached to the leg
loop of the rescuer's harness using a short
section of cord or webbing.

5. Girth Hitch separate slings through both the
victim's harness and the rescuer's harness,
and attach a locking carabiner to each sling.
These slings and locking carabiners are used
to anchor the rescuer and victim during multiple rappels.

6. Rappel down the rope and monitor the victim.

COUNTER-WEIGHT RAPPEL

The counter-weight rappel is a technique by which the rescuer and the victim descend the same rope, in close proximity, while counter-balancing one another. In essence, the rescuer is lowering the victim while rappelling on the same rope.

The counter-weight rappel, as with all techniques presented herein, must be practiced before it can be used in a rescue
situation. When practicing, the pretend victim and rescuer
should each have an independent safety rope and belayer.

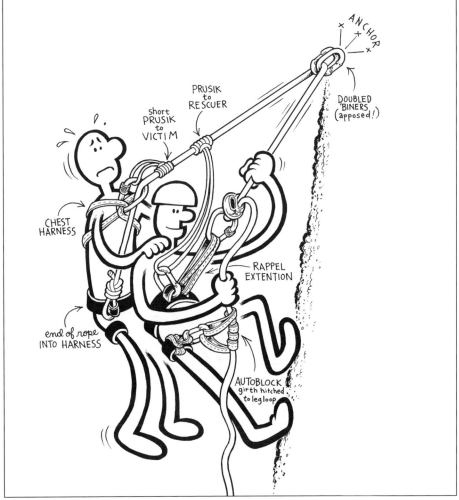

The labels in the illustration read:

ANCHOR

PRUSIK to RESCUER

short PRUSIK to VICTIM

DOUBLED BINERS (apposed!)

CHEST HARNESS

RAPPEL EXTENTION

end of rope INTO HARNESS

AUTOBLOCK girth hitched to leg loop

Single Rappel

The sequence is described assuming that the rescuer and the victim are both secured to a reliable rappel station. To anchor to the rappel station, use slings that have locking carabiners at each end and Girth Hitch the slings through each harness. The scenario also requires that the climbers share a rope and that the victim is tied into one end of the rope.

If the victim is injured or otherwise unable to assist in the rescue, you may have difficulty unclipping the victim from the anchor. In this instance, you may choose to attach the victim to the anchor with a Mariner knot. The rescuer will ease the victim's weight onto the Mariner knot and the sling with the locking carabiner that is Girth-hitched to the victim's harness should serve as backup. When attaching the victim to an anchor with a Mariner knot, if necessary, Girth Hitch two slings to ensure enough webbing to tie the Mariner Knot. If you use a cordelette to attach the victim, a Munter Mule Knot is preferred instead of a Mariner Knot.

Close up of counter-weight rappel setup. If the slings on the chest harness are too loose, slip one loop through the other and tie an overhand knot around both. Clip into the over-hand loop. I also like to add a short Prusik Knot from the carabiner to the rope. This Prusik holds the carabiner in place higher on the rope. This prevents the victim from slouching down.

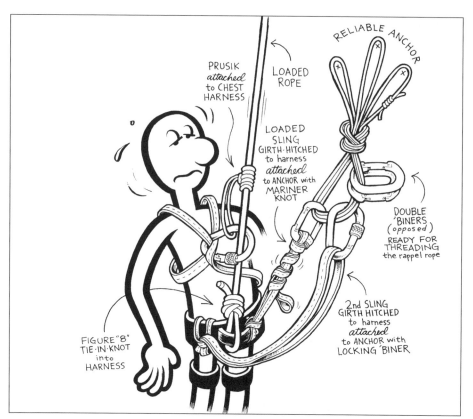

Close-up of how to anchor a victim during multiple counter-weight rappels.

Note: Rappels greater than half the length of the rope require two ropes to be tied together. Two differences in the technique arise when two ropes are used. First, the rescuer will need to pass a knot while rappelling (see description in Chapter 6). Second, the rescuer will need to untie the victim to retrieve the rope during multiple rappels.

During the single-rope counter-weight rappel, *the victim is always tied into one end of the rope,* and the rescuer is passing the slack rope through his rappel device.

Setup

1. Tie a Figure Eight knot at the end of the rope to prevent rappelling off the end. The loop of the Figure Eight will come in handy later and seldom comes undone.
2. *Optional* – Attach a chest harness made of two Girth-hitched slings to the victim. Secure the chest harness to the victim's end of the rope using a carabiner and friction knot.

Procedure

1. Attach a rappel device to the rescuer's side of the rope, under the anchor, and clip into it. To backup, extend your rappel device and attach an Autoblock knot below the rap-

pel device and connect it to your leg loop.

2. Tie a Mule knot with an overhand backup to lock the rappel device.

3. Attach a Prusik knot to the victim's side of the rope approximately half a meter from the victim's harness. If a chest harness is used, attach this Prusik knot above the knot connecting the chest harness to the rope.

4. Clip the other end of the Prusik knot to the *rescuer's harness.*

   Note: This Prusik knot will be under tension. Therefore, make sure the knot is clipped to the rescuer's harness through both the leg loop and the swami belt.

5. Unclip the victim from the anchors (Girth-hitched webbing and locking carabiner). Unload the Mariner knot and load the rescuer's rappel device and Mule knot.

6. Unload the Mule knot and load the rappel device.

7. Unclip from the anchors and rappel.

Options: Rappel side by side or, if the victim is injured, carry the victim piggyback during the rappel. To carry the victim piggyback, the Prusik knot running from the victim's side of the rope to your harness should be positioned in front of you. The section of rope between the Prusik knot and the victim's harness, as well as the victim, should be positioned over your shoulder and behind you.

MULTIPLE RAPPEL TRANSITION

Scenario: If you must pass more than one rappel station to reach the ground, the rescuer will need to build and connect himself/herself, and the victim, to a new anchor at each station. The rescuer will then need to retrieve the rope(s) and establish a new rappel.

1. Lock off the autoblock backup to stop the descent.

2. To backup, tie a Figure Eight Knot below your rappel device and clip it to your harness.

3. Set up the anchors for the next rappel.

4. If the victim is unable to assist, attach the victim to the rappel station with a Mariner or Munter Mule Knot.

5. Clip the victim into the rappel station with the sling and locking carabiner that is Girth-hitched to the victim's harness.

6. Clip yourself into the rappel station with the sling and locking carabiner that is Girth-hitched to your harness. Unload the Autoblock to weight the anchors.

7. Survey the scene. *The victim should remain tied into the rope.*

   Note: At this point consider continuing your descent using an Assisted Rappel. The Assisted Rappel is typically more efficient. If you wish to continue with a Counter Weight Rappel, proceed with steps 8 through 11.

8. Unclip the rappel device, *untie the knot at the end of the rope* (Figure Eight safety knot), and pull the rope through your previous rappel station.

   Note: If you are rappelling with two ropes tied together, you will need to untie the victim to retrieve the rope.

9. Tie a Figure Eight loop at the end of the rope to prevent rappelling off the end. Set up for the next rappel.

10. Attach your rappel device and tie a Mule knot.

11. Resume your rappel as explained in the counter-weight rappel section.

Leader Rescue CHAPTER 8

The objective of this section is to provide the reader with the framework of a safe system for a leader rescue. Various complications may arise, however, in which this system is not recommended. Be sure to survey the scene to determine what will work given the conditions.

Prior to attempting a leader rescue using The Five-Step Process or Counter-Weight Rappel Transition technique, the reliability of the top anchor or placement must be carefully considered. Unfortunately, in these scenarios, you will not be able to visually inspect or reinforce the top anchor or placement. However, you must have *complete confidence* that the top anchor will support both the victim and the additional weight of a climber ascending the rope. If, in your judgement, the top anchor is not completely reliable, *do not attempt to ascend to the victim*. You will endanger the victim, yourself, and possibly the lives of others.

Scenario: You are belaying a leader who falls near the top of a 150-foot pitch and is incapacitated by injuries. The leader is more than half a rope length from the belay, so there is not enough rope to lower the victim to the belay or ground.

Three leader-rescue methods are described in this section. The first is the Five-Step Process; the second is the Counter-weight Rappel Transition; the third is Assisting the Leader to Lower.

THE FIVE-STEP PROCESS

The basic sequence for The Five-Step Process involves the following:
1. Ascend to the victim.
2. Reinforce the anchors and attach the leader to the anchors.
3. Descend.
4. Re-ascend the rope.
5. Lower the victim.

Before beginning your sequence, you have to decide between two options – either lowering or raising the victim to a secure anchor.
- **First Option:** Lower the victim as close as possible to the best anchor position.
    Points to consider:
    a. The victim's injuries. It is not advisable to raise or lower an unconscious victim unless you are with the victim. The injuries may be compounded if the victim is hitting the rock as he/she is lowered.
    b. The estimated strength of the protection point you would like to lower the victim to.

Help Me!

c. The availability of backups near the protection point.

d. The amount of rope that can be fed out.

e. Ledges that may assist you in administering first aid.

f. The features of the pitch, such as the angle, protrusions or recesses, that may hinder the lowering.

• **Second Option:** Raise the victim to a better location to facilitate a rescue (i.e. a ledge with sold anchors just above the victim).

Establish a Z-pulley (described in Chapter 10) and raise the victim to a better location. Raising a victim is much more difficult and more time-consuming than lowering. Furthermore, a significant amount of force will be applied to the top piece of protection due to the forces generated by the pulley.

Step 1 – Ascend to the victim

1. Further reinforce your anchor for an upward pull.

2. Escape the belay using the Munter Mule combination, (described in Chapter 4). When tying the Figure Eight backup, allow at least one meter of slack. The slack will be used in Step 4 to tie a backup knot.

3. Girth Hitch a sling to your harness and attach a locking carabiner.

4. Ascend the rope to the leader using three friction knots – one for your foot and *two* for locking and self-belaying. The second friction knot is a backup.

Note: Due to tension in the rope created by the victim's weight, you will find the rope is more difficult to ascend than a slack rope. You also will be unable to tie backup Figure Eight knots. Clip the Girth-hitched sling and locking carabiner to the rope. While ascending the rope, unclip and re-clip protection points as you pass them. If your Prusik knots break or slip, the locking carabiner will catch a protection point to stop your fall.

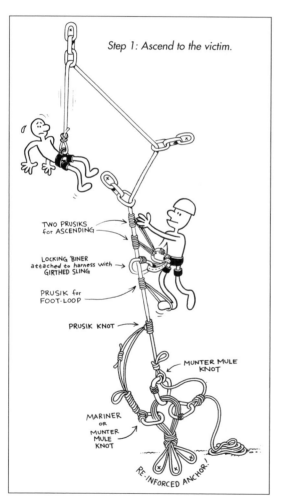

Step 1: Ascend to the victim.

TWO PRUSIKS for ASCENDING

LOCKING 'BINER attached to harness with GIRTHED SLING

PRUSIK for FOOT-LOOP

PRUSIK KNOT

MUNTER MULE KNOT

MARINER OR MUNTER MULE KNOT

RE-INFORCED ANCHOR!

Step 2 - Create an anchor and attach the leader

1. When you have reached the piece of protection you have selected to anchor the victim, build an anchor.

   Note: The piece of protection that caught the leader's fall, and any anchor you have lowered or raised the climber to, must be completely reliable. If these points are not reliable, you will need to build new anchors that are reliable.

2. Clip the victim to the anchor using a Mariner knot. If necessary, attach a chest harness to the victim.
3. Clip the victim directly to the anchor with a locking carabiner and a sling Girth-hitched to victim's harness. The load should be on the Mariner knot.
   - If the climb is a traverse, you may be unable to secure the victim directly to the nearest anchor because he is out of reach. If this is the case, the victim's end of the rope (versus the actual victim) can be secured to the nearest anchor using a Prusik and Mariner knot. This will secure the rope in place while the rescuer descends and re-ascends the rope.
4. Connect the rope you have just ascended to the anchor with a Prusik knot. The Prusik knot will load the anchors on a downward pull (their initial orientation) while you descend and re-ascend the rope.

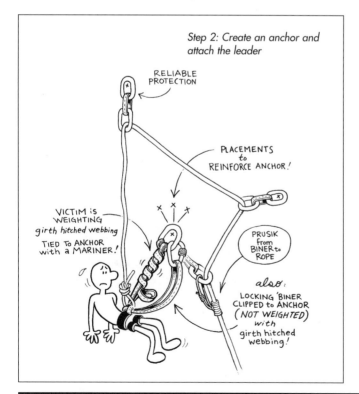

Step 2: Create an anchor and attach the leader

RELIABLE PROTECTION

PLACEMENTS to REINFORCE ANCHOR!

VICTIM is WEIGHTING girth hitched webbing TIED To ANCHOR with a MARINER!

PRUSIK from BINER to ROPE

also: LOCKING 'BINER CLIPPED to ANCHOR (NOT WEIGHTED) with girth hitched webbing!

Step 3 – Descend the rope

Basically, reverse the method of ascent – descending with three Prusik knots.

Step 4 – Re-ascend to the victim

1. To backup, attach a Figure Eight loop to your harness using the one meter of slack. Next, untie the backup Figure Eight knot that is attached to the bottom anchor.

2. Unload the bottom anchor by removing the Mariner knot, then the Munter Mule knot. In this instance the Mariner simply acts as another system backup.

3. Ascend the rope and clean the pitch. Backup regularly using Figure Eight loops clipped to your harness.

Note: Your weight will load the top Prusik knot. The weight of the victim is the backup for the Prusik knot. Be sure to leave any pieces of protection you may need as directionals or rappel stations.

4. Once you have reached the climber, clip into the anchor using the sling and locking carabiner Girth-hitched to your harness.

5. Backup with a Figure Eight loop attached to your harness. If the anchor you are weighting fails, any anchors above

Step 4: Remove original belay anchors and ascend to the victim.

RELIABLE PROTECTION

PRUSIK KNOT

GARDA HITCH *with* FOOT LOOP

BACK-UP FIGURE "8"

Step 5: Lower the victim.

RELIABLE PROTECTION

LOCKING 'BINER *attached to* harness *with* GIRTHED SLING

you – and the Figure Eight loop backup – will hold your fall. If you are clipped into the top anchor and it fails, the system will fail and you may die.

6. Remove the Prusik knots used for your ascent and the Prusik knot that was holding the rope.

7. At this point you will either lower the victim or rappel utilizing the assisted rappel or counter-weight rappel techniques explained in Chapter 7.

> *Note: The anchor that you have built to secure the victim should be absolutely reliable. Prior to lowering the victim, you should untie the victim, take in the slack, re-tie the victim and clip the rope through your new anchor. This adjustment is much safer because you no longer will have to rely on the top piece of protection, which you may not have inspected. This technique is detailed in the "Variation to the Five-Step Process" section below.*

Step 5 – Lower the victim

Prior to lowering, check that the victim is conscious and responsive. The lowering procedure may further injure the victim by jarring and scraping the victim against the rock. If the victim is not responsive, or has serious injuries, an assisted or counter-weight rappel will be necessary so you can accompany the victim down.

With a conscious victim, you can use the procedure described below. Make sure the rope is running through the anchor above you. You will be lowering the victim to the ground using your belay device.

1. Tie a Mule knot to lock your belay device.
2. Tie a knot at the end of the rope.
3. Unclip the sling that is Girth-hitched from the victim's harness to the anchor. Clip the carabiner to the victim's harness.
4. Untie and unload the Mariner knot. This will load the rescuer's belay device and the Mule knot.
5. Untie and unload the Mule knot.
6. Lower the victim to the ground. If the rope does not reach the ground, adjust the rope or establish multiple rappels. A rope adjustment is explained in the following section.

Variation to the Five-Step Process

In some cases, rope adjustments are necessary to complete the rescue. The variation that allows you to make such adjustments is described below.

Scenario: You ascend to the victim, and there is not enough rope to lower the victim to the ground. The leader has fallen past several pieces of protection. Much of the rope is above, running through pieces of protection placed higher on the climb by the leader. However, if you can increase the amount of rope available to you, the victim can be lowered to the ground.

You and the victim must be attached to the same anchor by slings that have been Girth-hitched to your harnesses. Furthermore, the rope must have been released from the bottom anchor to allow the lowering.

1. Reinforce the anchor. The anchor must be absolutely secure. If it's not, lower to a more suitable point and build a new anchor.

2. Clip the rope to your harness so it is not dropped accidentally. Next, untie the victim from the end of the rope and pull the rope through the piece or pieces of protection above.

3. Re-tie the victim to the end of the rope and clip the rope through the anchors.

4. Tie a knot at the end of the rope.

5. Adjust the slack and lower the victim.

Warning! If the anchor fails, you will not have any backups.

COUNTER-WEIGHT RAPPEL TRANSITION

Scenario: You are prepared to ascend the rope to anchor the victim. However, you are on a route that does not offer a suitable anchor point convenient to the victim. This section describes how you would ascend to the victim and prepare a counter-weight rappel.

Warning! This method assumes that the top piece of protection can withstand the forces typically applied to a reliable anchor. However, you may not be able to inspect or backup this protection point. If, in your judgement, the top piece of protection is not absolutely reliable, do not attempt this method.

1. Escape the belay and ascend to the victim as previously described.

2. Once you have reached the victim, secure a Prusik knot to the rope you have just ascended, above the highest Prusik you used to ascend the rope.

3. Secure this new Prusik to either:
• the loop formed buy the Figure Eight follow-through on the victim's harness (for added safety, two Prusiks are show in the illustration); or
• another Prusik knot tied to the rope weighted by the victim at a point a half-meter above the victim. Using a carabiner, attach the opposing Prusik knots together.

4. Descend and remove your original belay anchors.

5. Ascend the rope to the victim.

6. Set up a counter-weight rappel and descend.

Note: By attaching Prusik knots, the victim will remain in the same location while the rescuer descends and re-ascends the rope.

A second technique for setting up a counter-weight rappel.

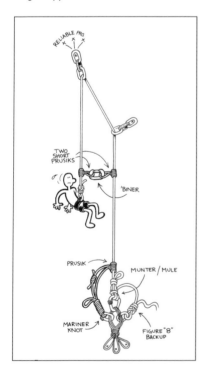

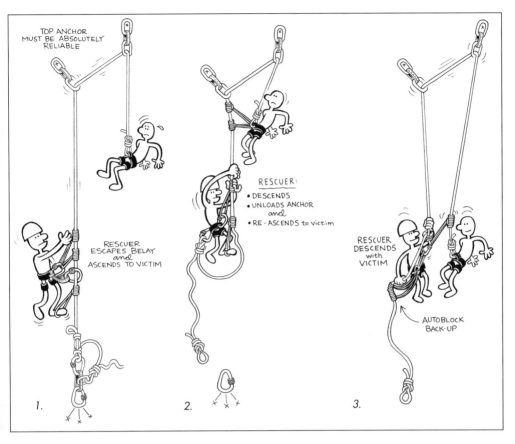

The three steps to setting up a counter-weight transition.

ASSISTING THE LEADER TO LOWER

Scenario: You are belaying a leader who has been injured during a fall, or is simply backing off a route, and you wish to lower the climber. Due to the length of the pitch, there is not enough rope to lower the leader to the ground. The climber is able to assist, but his unstable position requires the belayer to remain in control of the rope.

1. Lower the leader to the closest reliable piece of protection.

2. The leader backs up the protection point and anchors to it with a sling and locking carabiner that is Girth-hitched to his harness.

3. Once the leader is anchored, feed out one meter of slack.

4. The leader clips the slack rope through the anchor, ties a Figure Eight loop, and attaches it to his harness using two opposite/opposing carabiners. The leader is still on belay.

5. The leader unties his original tie-in knot and pulls the rope from the top piece.

6. Next, the leader reties to the end of the rope, clips the rope through the anchor and unties the Figure Eight loop.

7. The belayer takes in the slack until the rope is taut.

8. The leader unclips from the anchor and is lowered by his belayer.

Assisting the leader to lower.

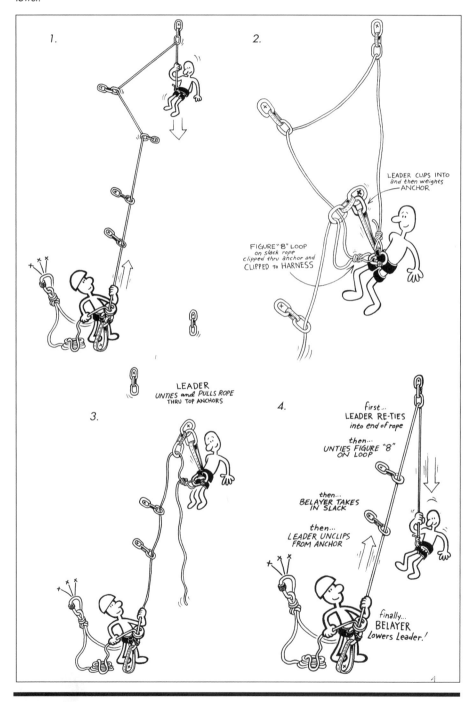

1.

2.

LEADER CLIPS INTO
and then weights
ANCHOR

FIGURE "8" LOOP
on slack rope
clipped thru anchor and
CLIPPED TO HARNESS

LEADER
UNTIES and PULLS ROPE
THRU TOP ANCHORS

3.

4.

first...
LEADER RE-TIES
into end of rope

then...
UNTIES FIGURE "8"
ON LOOP

then...
BELAYER TAKES
IN SLACK

then...
LEADER UNCLIPS
FROM ANCHOR

finally...
BELAYER
Lowers Leader!

Rescuing the Second

CHAPTER 9

This chapter describes two techniques for rescuing the second climber.

The first technique is to lower the injured climber with assistance using a counterweight and Assited Rappel. The second technique uses an assisted hoist to raise a climber that is injured or simply unable to ascend past a difficult section.

Scenario: You have led a pitch and anchored in. You are belaying your partner up the pitch and he/she is injured while climbing. Due to the injuries and nature of the route, you wish to descend with the victim in close proximity. You need to reach your partner, administer first aid, and rappel to the ground. If the victim is in good condition and an assisted or counter-weight rappel is not necessary, you can simply lower the victim to the ground.

Three situations will be described in this chapter:

- **Situation 1:** The victim is less than half a rope-length away and a new anchor is not required.
- **Situation 2:** The victim is less than half a rope-length away and a new anchor must be built for you to reach the ground.
- **Situation 3:** The victim is more than half a rope-length away and a new anchor needs to be built for you to reach the ground.

Situation 1

In this case, the victim is less than half a rope-length away and a new anchor is not required.

1. Descend to the victim by escaping the belay and positioning the rope so it will be set up for a counter-weight rappel. At this point the rope is loaded to a Mariner or Mule Knot with a Prusik. To backup, attach a Figure Eight loop to the anchor.
2. Set up your rappel device on the loose rope. Tie off your rappel device with a Mule knot and overhand.
3. Untie from the rope, tie a Figure Eight knot at the end of the rope, and lower the rope.
4. A this point three different methods may be used:
   - Mariner knot release: Untie the backup

Yow!

*Rescuing the second
using a variation to the
counter-weight rappel.*

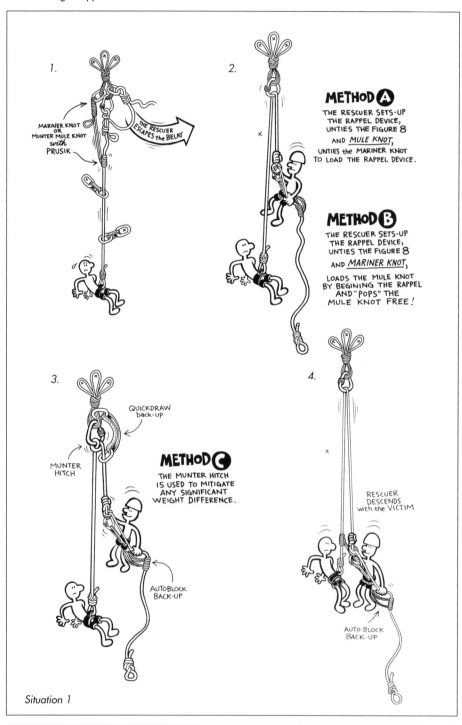

1.

MARINER KNOT
OR
MUNTER MULE KNOT
with
PRUSIK

THE RESCUER
ESCAPES the BELAY

2.

METHOD A

THE RESCUER SETS-UP
THE RAPPEL DEVICE,
UNTIES THE FIGURE 8
AND *MULE KNOT*,
UNTIES the MARINER KNOT
TO LOAD THE RAPPEL DEVICE.

METHOD B

THE RESCUER SETS-UP
THE RAPPEL DEVICE,
UNTIES THE FIGURE 8
AND *MARINER KNOT*,
LOADS THE MULE KNOT
BY BEGINING THE RAPPEL
AND "POPS" THE
MULE KNOT FREE !

3.

QUICKDRAW
back-up

MUNTER
HITCH

METHOD C

THE MUNTER HITCH
IS USED TO MITIGATE
ANY SIGNIFICANT
WEIGHT DIFFERENCE.

AUTOBLOCK
BACK-UP

4.

RESCUER
DESCENDS
with the VICTIM

AUTO BLOCK
BACK-UP

Situation 1

Figure Eight. To load your rappel device, untie the Mule knot used to lock your rappel device in place. The victim's weight is on the Mariner knot. Untie the Mariner knot to load the rappel device.

The advantage using the Mariner knot to descend is that it is already loaded and easily released. The disadvantage is that the weight of the victim may (although rarely) pull you into the rappel anchors when the knot is released.

- Mule knot release: To load your rappel device, untie the Mariner knot used to escape the belay. The victim's weight is on the Mule knot used to lock your rappel device in place. Untie the backup Figure Eight. Weight the Mule knot to load the rappel device. Once weighted, untie the Mule Knot and it will "pop" free to load your rappel device.

The advantage of the Mule knot is that it allows for a very quick transition.

- Munter Mule knot release: Escape the belay and tie a Munter Mule Knot to the rappel anchor using the main rope. To load your rappel device, untie the Mariner knot used to escape the belay. The victim's weight is now on the Munter Mule knot. Untie the backup Figure Eight. Untie the Mule Knot used to lock your rappel device. Weight the Munter Mule knot to load the rappel device. Once weighted, the Mule knot will release and the Munter Hitch will mitigate the weight difference, allowing you to reach the victim. The victim's rope should be on the load side of the Munter Hitch.

The advantage of using the Munter Mule Knot is that it will mitigate any weight difference and prevent you from being pulled into the anchors. This disadvantage is that the knot increases the potential for getting the rope stuck when you retrieve your rappel rope. You will also need to leave a locking pear style carabiner at the rappel station.

5. When you reach the victim, administer first aid if needed.
6. Secure a Prusik knot to the victim's rope and attach the other end to your harness.
7. Continue to descend using a counter-weight rappel.

Note: The above mentioned techniques assume you are belaying with a waist belay. However, if you use a re-directed belay, the escape and rescue takes a mere ten seconds! Simply unclip from the anchors (you are attached to the system with your belay device) and rappel to the victim. Stop your descent by wrapping the rope around your thigh and set up the counter weight rappel.

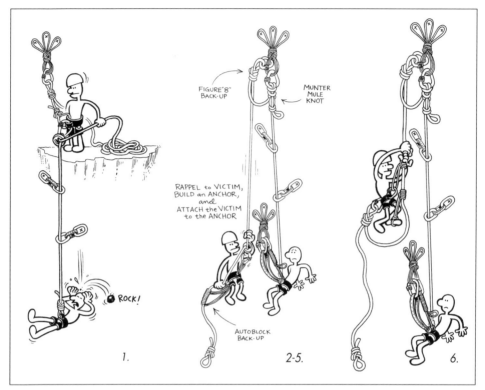

FIGURE 8"
BACK-UP

MUNTER
MULE
KNOT

RAPPEL to VICTIM,
BUILD an ANCHOR,
and
ATTACH the VICTIM
to the ANCHOR

● ROCK!

AUTOBLOCK
BACK-UP

1.

2-5.

6.

Rescuing the second using the setup described in Situation 2.

Situation 2

In this scenario, the victim is less than half a rope-length away and a new anchor must be built to reach the ground.

1. Escape the belay and position the rope so that you can rappel to the victim.
2. Attach your rappel device and lock it off with a Mule Knot and Overhand. Untie from the rope, tie a knot at the end ad lower the rope.
3. Rappel down the slack rope. While rappelling down the rope, you are loading the backup Figure Eight knot attached to the anchor.
4. Descend to the victim. Administer first aid; if necessary, rig a chest harness for the victim and attach it to the rope using a friction knot.
5. Construct a new anchor and attach the victim to that anchor.

   Note: It may be easier to construct a new anchor before you reach the victim. In this case, you would secure the loaded rope to the new anchor with Prusik and Mariner knots. This method is detailed in Situation 3, which is described below.

6. Ascend to the top anchor, set up your rappel device on the loose rope, tie off your rappel device with a Mule knot and overhand.

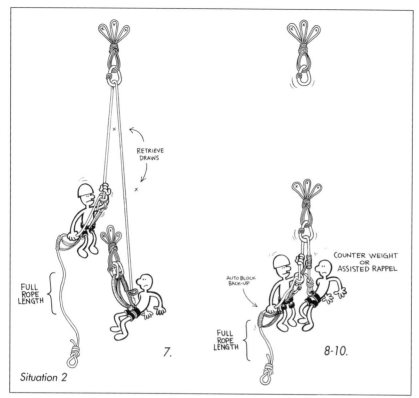

RETRIEVE
DRAWS

FULL
ROPE
LENGTH

COUNTER WEIGHT
OR
ASSISTED RAPPEL

AUTO BLOCK
BACK-UP

FULL
ROPE
LENGTH

7.

8-10.

Situation 2

7. Use one of the previously described methods, Mariner Knot, Mule Knot, or Munter Mule to descend to the victim.
8. When you reach the victim, secure yourself to the new anchor.
9. Retrieve the rope to establish a rappel off the anchor you are tied into.
10. Use the assisted or counter-weight rappel techniques (described in Chapter 7) to reach the ground.

Situation 3

The victim is greater than half a rope-length away and a new anchor must be built.
1. Escape the belay and position the rope so that you can rappel to the victim.
2. Attach your rappel device and lock it off with a Mule Knot and Overhand. Untie from the rope, tie a knot at the end and lover the rope.
3. Rappel down the slack rope. While rappelling down the rope, you are loading the backup Figure Eight knot.
4. Once you have reached the end of the slack rope, attach two Prusik knots to the victim's loaded rope and continue to descend on the loaded rope.
Optional—Backup by clipping the loaded rope with a locking carabiner attached to a sling that is Girth-hitched to your harness.

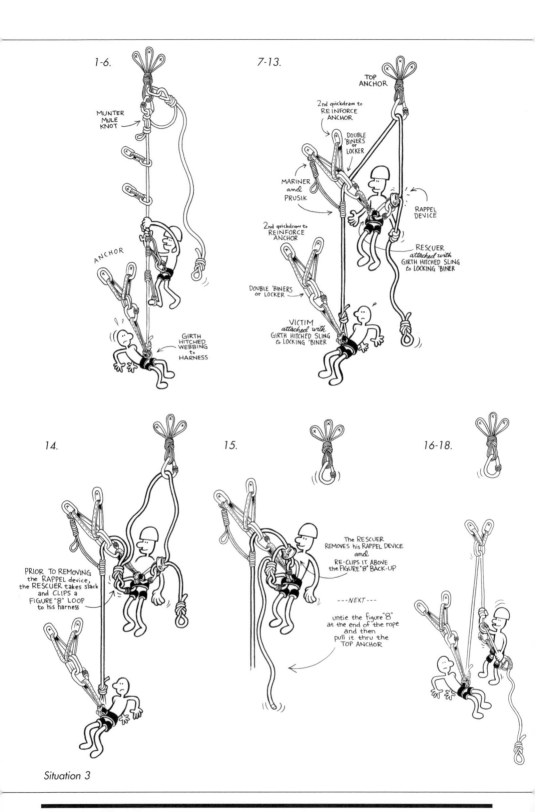

Situation 3

5. Descend to the victim. Administer first aid. If necessary, rig a chest harness for the victim and attach it to the rope using a friction knot.
6. Construct a new anchor and attach the victim to that anchor.
7. Ascend the loaded rope to the loose rappel rope. Clip into the Figure Eight knot at the end of the rope. Transfer your Prusiks to the slack rope.
8. From this point, ascend the slack rope at least three meters.
9. Build an anchor and secure the loaded rope, which is holding the victim, to the anchor with Prusik and Mariner knots.
10. Ascend to the top anchor.
11. Use one of the previously described methods, Mariner Knot, Mule Knot, or Munter Mule to descend.
12. Rappel to the newly constructed anchor, retrieving gear placed on the lead, and clip into the anchor.

Rappel Station Transition

13. Double-check that the Prusik and Mariner knots, which are attached from the anchor to the loaded rope, are both secure.
14. System backup—Take a segment of rope that is running through your new rappel station and use it to attach a Figure Eight loop to your harness.
15. Remove your rappel device and pull the rope through the top anchor.
16. Set up your next rappel using the Autoblock backup by placing your rappel device above the Figure Eight backup knot.
17. Remove the backup Figure Eight loop. Next, release the Mariner and the Prusik knots from the rope.
18. Rappel to the victim.
19. When you reach the victim, adjust the rope for an assisted or counter-weight rappel (described in Chapter 7) to the ground.

Note: The rappel station transition decribed in steps 14-18 may be greatly simplified. When yo reach the new rappel station, clip in and remove your rappel device. Next, pull the rope through the top anchor and continue your rappel to the victim. However, this asumes that, as luck would have it, the protection points you originally attached the victim to are adequate for a new rappel station. Typically, the pieces you have attached the victim to are suitable to stabalize the victim's position, but they do not meet the criteria for an anchor. A suitable anchor will be established after further lowering the victim to an area which has better anchor placements. Therefore, the above system is described because it has extra precautions built in. These extra precautions are taken in case the piece(s) that the victim is attached to fail.

(page opposite)
Transition to a new rappel station when the victim is greater than a half-rope length from the rescuer.

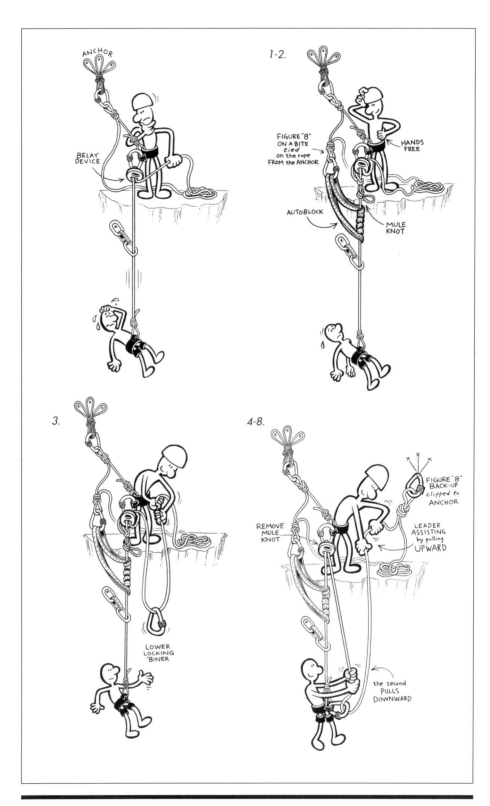

ASSISTED HOIST

Scenario: You have led a pitch and anchored in. Your partner is unable to climb a section of the route and needs to be hoisted up a section. To use this method, the second must be a fully functioning climber who is less than 50 feet below the belay.

If your partner is more than 50 feet away, or there is more than one-third of your rope between the two of you, the climber should ascend the rope with Prusik knots.

The procedure goes like this:

1. Tie a Mule knot with an overhand backup to free your hands.
2. Attach an Autoblock knot to the loaded rope, below the belay device and toward the victim, and attach it to your anchors. The Autoblock can be freed while loaded, which is an advantage in this situation.
3. Clip a locking carabiner to a coil of rope and lower it to the climber, who should clip the carabiner to his/her harness.

Note: If the victim pulls on the slack rope, the Mule knot will release prematurely if not backed up with an Overhand.

4. Take in the slack and attach the rope to the anchors with a Figure Eight on a bight. Untie the overhand above the Mule knot.

Note: In the illustration, a separate anchor has been built for the backup Figure Eight. A separate anchor is not needed for this technique; it has been used in the illustration for clarity.

5. Tell the climber to pull on the slack rope. The second may also want to attach Prusik knots to the slack rope to assist when he/she pulls down on the rope.
6 Untie the Overhand backup. Once the climber applies pressure to the slack rope, the Mule knot will "pop" free.
7 Take in the slack formed as the second ascends, while also monitoring the Autoblock. This is essential as it has taken the place of the belayer's brake hand.
8. Your partner hoists himself/herself up by pulling down on the slack rope. The belayer will assist by pulling upward.
9. If the climber ascends more than 15 feet, lock the Autoblock and tie another Figure Eight backup and clip it to the anchor.
10. Once the climber has ascended past the obstacle, load the Autoblock knot and place your brake hand and guide hand back in position. Ask the second to unclip the rope that was lowered.
11. Take in the slack.
12. When your partner resumes climbing, unlock the Autoblock and continue belaying the climber up the pitch.

Opposite page: The steps to an assisted hoist.

On the rocks.

Jim Detterline photo

Pulley Systems

CHAPTER   10

This section describes in detail the basic construction of pulley systems, which enable a rescuer to raise a victim. The pully system is also an important tool used to unload a knot that is jammed in a system. The systems I have chosen to include are the classic Z-pulley and the 5:1 pulley. The Z-pulley was chosen because it is a simple system to remember and construct. However, if you are alone and attempt to haul a victim using the Z-pulley, you'll find it extremely difficult. Therefore, the 5:1 pulley is also described.

The number of times a machine multiplies a force of effort is called its "mechanical advantage." The theoretical mechanical advantage of the Z-pulley is 3 to 1, which means that by using the Z-pulley, the belayer has three times the power he/she would have if working without one. However, when improvising these systems the actual advantage is much lower. Before using a pulley system, always take into account, and compensate for, the increased force that will be placed on the entire system!

Before raising a victim with the Z-pulley, make sure the victim is able to talk to you. Raising an unresponsive victim is not recommended unless you can monitor the victim from a close proximity. Raising an unresponsive victim may compound their injuries.

Note: Whenever possible, try to avoid raising a victim. It is a very strenuous activity. Although the Z-pulley increases the mechanical advantage of the raising system, you still might be unable to raise the victim without assistance. The 5:1 pulley gives you an even greater advantage and is explained in the section following the Z-pulley. However, you should master the basic Z-pulley before learning the more complicated 5:1 pulley system.

RAISING A VICTIM WITH A Z-PULLEY

Scenario: You have just led a pitch and anchored in. While you are belaying, your second is injured and can not ascend the pitch. (Assume the victim can clean the protection). Your objective is to raise the victim with a Z-pulley. A Munter Mule and Prusik combination, as well as a standard Prusik, are illustrated to demonstrate a variety of options.

To set up and use a Z-pulley system:
1. Tie a Mule knot with an overhand backup to free your hands.
2. Take three meters of slack and tie a Figure Eight loop. Clip the loop to your anchors. Attach two more carabiners to the anchors to rotate backup knots – the same backup procedure as for ascending a rope.

3. Tie a "ratcheting" friction knot. Each time you raise the victim with the Z-pulley, you will slide the "ratcheting" friction knot down the rope to hold the victim while adjusting the pulley.

Attach the "ratcheting" friction knot – typically a Prusik knot – from the anchor to the loaded rope. This knot should be attached to the rope as far as you can comfortably reach. Two methods are shown.

4. Untie the Mule knot and transfer the load to the ratcheting friction knot.
5. Escape from the belay.
6. You have three options when creating the system once you escape the belay. You should practice each of them :
   - **Option 1:** Attach your belay device and locking carabiner to the anchor.
   - **Option 2:** Remove your belay device to prevent it from accidentally locking or getting in the way. Once removed, clip the rope through your locking carabiner or two opposite and opposed carabiners.
   - **Option 3:** Clip the rope through two matching, oval carabiners to form a Garda Hitch. The Garda Hitch will hold the weight of the climber, especially if the rope is icy and the ratcheting friction knot is slipping. However, the hauling system will be less efficient due to the resistance created by the Garda Hitch.

The four drawings below illustrate methods of attaching a ratcheting friction knot. Picture 3a illustrates raising a victim using a cordelette; 3b shows a belay escape using the main rope and a Prusik.

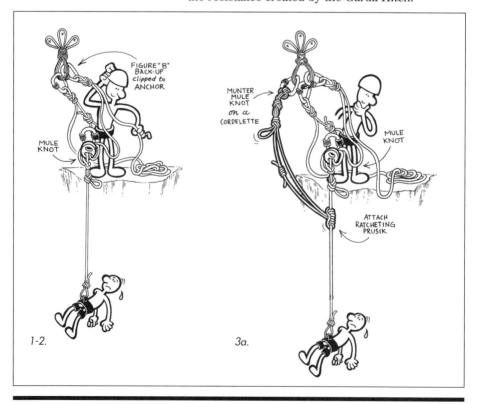

7. Attach a locking Prusik to the loaded rope. This Prusik loop is used to create the pulley. The hauling system will be more efficient if you use a short piece of cord to tie the locking Prusik knot.

Note: If you place the locking Prusik knot above the ratcheting friction knot, as opposed to beneath it, you do not have to monitor the ratcheting friction knot. However, it may prove less efficient because you need to haul in shorter increments.

You have two options when attaching the locking Prusik:
- **Option 1** – Attach the locking Prusik above the originally loaded ratcheting friction knot, toward the belayer and away from the victim, and clip a carabiner through the cord.
- **Option 2** – The standard method involves placing the locking Prusik below the ratcheting friction knot. In this case, the ratcheting Prusik is positioned close to the anchor.

Note: I have had success when I run the rope through a Black Diamond ATC (a commonly used belay device) and attach the locking Prusik below my ratcheting Prusik (toward the victim). The ATC prevents the ratcheting Prusik from feeding into the anchor and jamming. When slack is released, the ratcheting Prusik holds the rope in place.

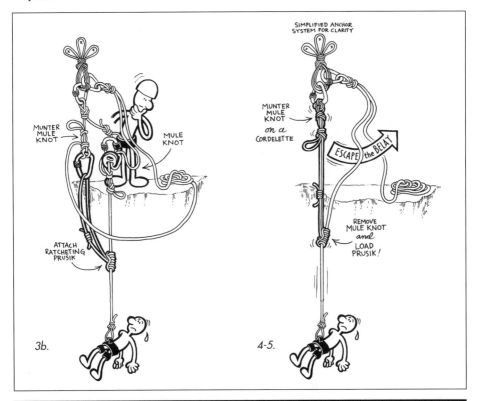

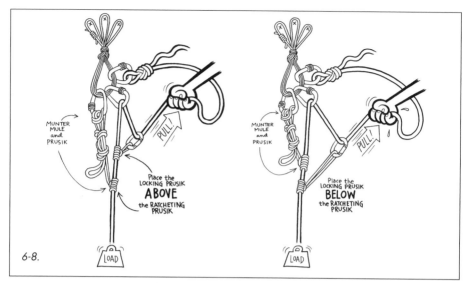

MUNTER MULE and PRUSIK

Place the LOCKING PRUSIK
ABOVE
the RATCHETING PRUSIK

MUNTER MULE and PRUSIK

Place the LOCKING PRUSIK
BELOW
the RATCHETING PRUSIK

6-8.

LOAD

LOAD

Two options for attaching the ratcheting Prusik knot in a Z-pulley system.

8. Clip the slack end of the rope through the carabiner attached to the locking Prusik knot. You have just created a classic Z-pulley, which provides a theoretical 3-to-1 mechanical advantage.

Raising the Victim with the Z-pulley

Several simple steps enable you to raise the victim.
1. To raise the victim, pull the slack rope toward the anchor until the locking Prusik knot is touching the anchor.
2. Load the ratcheting friction knot by sliding the knot down the rope (toward the victim). Slowly release some slack until the Prusik knot locks.
3. Adjust the locking Prusik knot by sliding the knot down the rope (toward the victim). Repeat steps 1 and 2 until you have lifted the climber to safety.

To release a loaded friction knot from an anchor:

Releasing a loaded friction knot involves the following:
1. Adjust the backup Figure Eight knot to prevent shock-loading the system if the friction knot fails or slips.
2. Clip a carabiner through the friction knot. A space is provided by the carabiner that attaches the friction knot to the anchor.
3. Attach the carabiner to the anchor with another carabiner and a Mariner knot.
4. Pull on the rope to load the locking Prusik knot, and unclip the friction knot from the anchor.
5. Load the Mariner knot and friction knot by letting out slack.
6. Remove the locking Prusik knot from the rope.
7. Clip a locking carabiner to the anchor and attach a belay device or tie a Munter Hitch. Tie a Mule knot and overhand backup.

(page opposite) Releasing a loaded ratcheting knot.

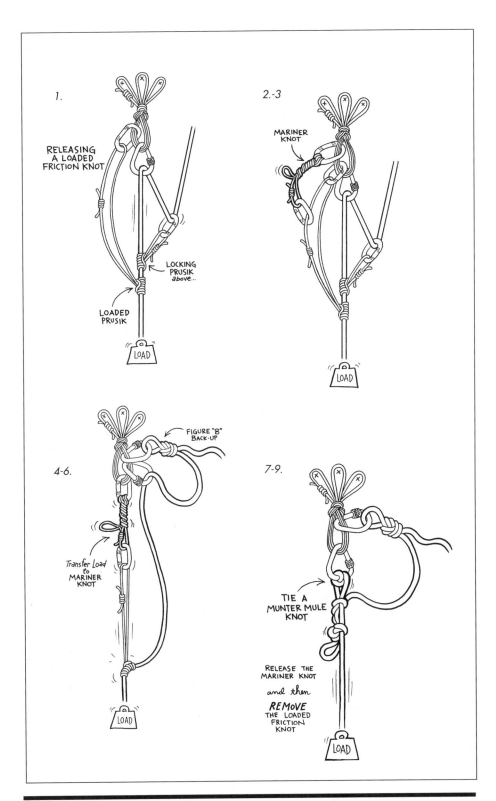

1.

RELEASING
A LOADED
FRICTION KNOT

LOCKING
PRUSIK
above...

LOADED
PRUSIK

LOAD

2.-3

MARINER
KNOT

LOAD

4-6.

FIGURE "8"
BACK-UP

Transfer Load to
MARINER
KNOT

LOAD

7-9.

TIE A
MUNTER MULE
KNOT

RELEASE THE
MARINER KNOT

and then

REMOVE
THE LOADED
FRICTION
KNOT

LOAD

8. Untie the Mariner knot and load the Mule knot and belay device or Munter Hitch.
9. Remove the Prusik knot and sling from the Mariner knot.

To unload a Garda Hitch used with a Z-pulley:

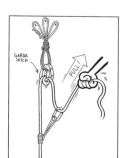

3:1 pulley system with a Garda Hitch.

A Garda Hitch can be used in place of the ratcheting friction knot in a Z-pulley system. The Garda Hitch can be set up very quickly and, with practice, takes less time to monitor that a ratcheting friction knot. However, the Garda Hitch will add some resistance to the pulley system, which will decrease its mechanical advantage.

This is a good hitch to use when you need to haul a small pack. As with any pulley system, backup frequently with Figure Eights.

1. Adjust the Figure Eight backup knot to prevent shock-loading the anchors if the new ratcheting Prusik or Mariner knots (see step 3) fail or slip.
2. Secure a ratcheting Prusik knot to the loaded rope.
3. Attach the new ratcheting Prusik knot to the anchor with a Mariner knot (employ the method previously described in the section "To release a loaded friction knot from an anchor").
4. While pulling on the rope to raise the victim, place a spare carabiner or nut tool between the Garda Hitch carabiners to loosen the hitch.
5. The nut tool keeps the Garda Hitch from pinching the rope as you raise the victim. This also allows you to let out slack through the hitch and transfer the load to the ratcheting Prusik knot.
6. Remove the rope from the Garda Hitch. Transfer the load from the Mariner knot to a Mule knot as previously described on page 78.

THE 5-TO-1 PULLEY SYSTEM

The great advantage of the 3:1 Z-pulley system is its simplicity. However, if you attempt to haul a victim by yourself using a Z-pulley, you'll find it is extremely difficult. If you need to haul a victim by yourself, use the 5:1 pulley system. In my opinion, this system is the easiest of the more complicated systems to construct.

The following narrative will not provide a detailed task analysis. Please refer to the illustration provided in this section when constructing the 5:1 pulley You'll also find an illustration showing a 7:1 pulley system. If you are interested in learning how to set up more advanced systems, as well as the physics involved in those systems, *Wilderness Search and Rescue,* by Tim J. Setnicka, is a very good source.

Setup

1. Attach the locking Prusik knot to the loaded rope as far away as you can comfortably reach. The protruding loop on the Prusik should be as short as possible.
2. Attach a ratcheting friction knot to the rope exactly between the locking Prusik and the point where the rope runs through the anchor.
3. You will need a separate section of cord or webbing to create the 5:1 advantage. I have had the most success using a double-length (44-inch long), sewn, ⁵⁄₁₆-inch runner.
4. When constructed properly, the ratcheting Prusik will reach the anchor at the same moment the carabiners used to construct the pulley come into contact. While the carabiners are in contact, the ratcheting friction knot is easier to adjust.

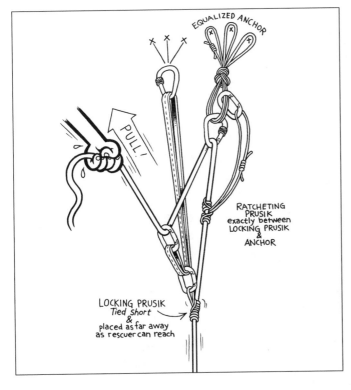

Setting up a 5:1 pulley system.

Setting up a 7:1 pulley system.

The Hesse-Brandler,
Cima Grande,
Dolomites, Italy

Photo: Jim Dockery

Aid Climbing

Aid climbing is *briefly* described in this manual to complement the rescuer's skills. Aid climbing involves the use of equipment to ascend and protect a fall. A situation may arise where you may need to aid climb or aid solo to complete a pitch.

This is an example of one system used by aid climbers. It has the advantage of being easy and efficient. Also, the carabiners connected to your aiders and daisy chain will not shift when you weight the aiders.

The disadvantage of this system is its appetite for carabiners. You may need to back-clean to replenish your supply. You also may drop gear accidentally if it is not connected to a daisy chain.

Setup

To set up for aid climbing, you must:

1. Improvise aiders, if you don't have them, by Girth-hitching slings together. An aider or e'trier basically is a step ladder made of nylon. Attach a carabiner to each aider.
2. Girth hitch a sling or daisy chain to your harness and attach a carabiner to the end. If you have extra webbing, two slings or daisy chains are recommended.
3. Girth hitch a short sling to your harness and attach a Fifi Hook or carabiner. If you have a belay loop on the front of your harness you can simply attach a carabiner to the belay loop and use the carabiner as your Fifi Hook.

Sequence

One sequence for utilizing aid climbing technique to overcome a difficult section of a climb is as follows:

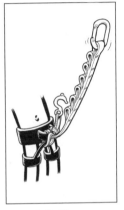

An aid climbing setup.

1. Place a piece of protection and clip a quickdraw to it.
2. Clip one of the aiders to the top carabiner of the quickdraw. You may prefer to clip your daisy chain to the piece before your aiders.
3. Clip your daisy chain to the top carabiner of the aider or into one of the steps in the aider.
4. Test the piece by weighting and bouncing.
5. If the piece holds, climb the aider and hook in with your Fifi Hook or carabiner.
6. Clip the rope through the bottom carabiner of the quickdraw.
7. Weight the Fifi Hook (or carabiner), retrieve the aiders from your last placement. Relax and plan your next placement.
8. Place a piece of protection and clip a quickdraw to it.
9. Clip the second aider to the top carabiner of the quickdraw.
10. Clip your daisy chain to the top carabiner of the aider or into one of the steps in the aider.
11. Release your Fifi Hook and repeat steps 4 through 10 to ascend.

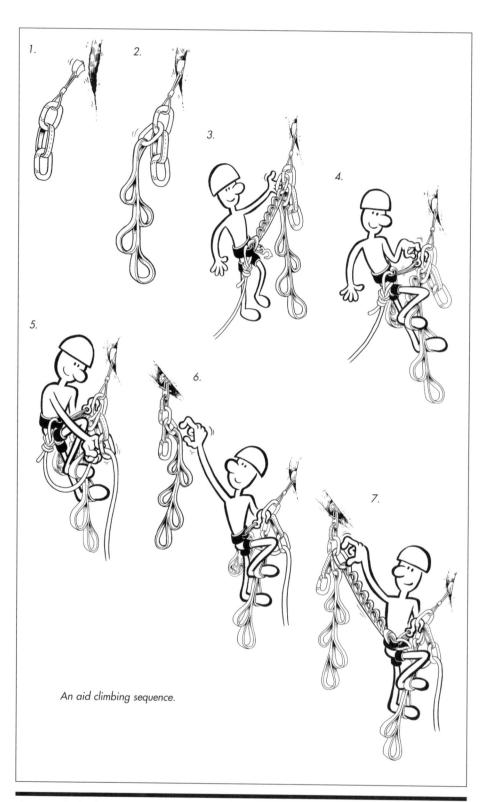

1.

2.

3.

4.

5.

6.

7.

An aid climbing sequence.

AID SOLOING

Aid soloing is aid climbing using a self-belay system. The self-belay system described in is book is the Clove Hitch method. The Clove Hitch method utilizes very little equipment and is easy to use once you have practiced. However aid soling, as with most of the skills described in this book, is an advanced climbing technique.

I strongly advise seeking qualified, hands-on instruction to supplement the sequence described in this book.

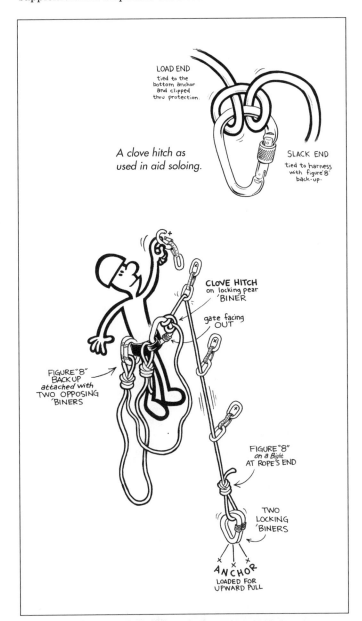

LOAD END
tied to the
bottom anchor
and clipped
thru protection.

*A clove hitch as
used in aid soloing.*

SLACK END
tied to harness
with figure 8"
back-up.

CLOVE HITCH
on locking pear
'BINER

gate facing
OUT

FIGURE "8"
BACK UP
attached with
TWO OPPOSING
'BINERS

FIGURE "8"
on a Bight
AT ROPE'S END

TWO
LOCKING
'BINERS

ANCHOR
LOADED FOR
UPWARD PULL

An aid-soloing setup.

Warning! Aid soloing can be very dangerous. Practice with a separate rope and backup belayer before relying on this technique.

Setup

Begin with the following three steps:

- At the start of the pitch, anchor one end of the rope to a bombproof, multi-directional anchor.
- Tie into the other end of the rope.
- Attach a locking pear-shaped carabiner to the front of your harness. Attach two sets of opposing carabiners (or two lockers) to your harness.

1. *From the bottom anchor,* measure four meters of rope and tie a Figure Eight loop.

2. Backup by clipping the Figure Eight loop with two opposing carabiners to your harness.

3. *From the bottom anchor,* measure two meters of rope and tie a Clove Hitch to the locking carabiner.

4. Begin aid climbing the pitch. While leading you will be clipping the section of rope under the Clove Hitch to your placements.

Note: In theory, you are placing pieces as for a typical aid lead. If you fall or a piece fails, your weight will lock the Clove Hitch and the last piece will catch your fall. The Clove Hitch works best here because it is easily adjusted.

5. When the rope becomes taut to the Clove Hitch, readjust the Clove Hitch to pay out the amount of slack you feel comfortable with.

6. When the rope becomes taut on the Figure Eight loop, take 3 meters of slack and tie a new Figure Eight loop. Attach it to your harness with the second set of opposing carabiners.

7. Unclip and untie the previous Figure Eight loop and continue climbing. Readjust the Clove Hitch and the Figure Eight backups as necessary.

Note: This method can also be used to protect a free climber. Using the same process described above, you will be free climbing instead of aid climbing. However, using this method while free climbing is very cumbersome due to the amount of rope adjustments required to pay out slack and reposition your backup knots.

Evacuating the Victim

This manual does not describe detailed emergency care procedures. I highly recommend first-aid training from one of the organizations listed in the appendix. These organizations supplement traditional first-aid training with backcountry first aid.

The following is a brief list of steps the rescuers should follow during an evacuation.

Survey the Scene

The objective is to prevent further injuries by assessing the environment to identify potential risks to the rescuer, bystanders or victim.

The Patient Exam

Conduct a physical examination of the victim to the extent of your first aid training to determine his/her status.

- Once satisfied the scene is safe, check the victim's ABCs – Airway, Breathing, and Circulation.
- Next, perform a head-to-toe hands-on patient exam. Always suspect serious neck injuries and be prepared to treat for shock.
- As soon as time permits, prepare a "SOAP" note. You should record and monitor the following information:
  - **Subjective** – age, sex, mechanism of injury, chief complaint, description of pain.
  - **Objective** – vital signs, patient exam, patient history (e.g. "SAMPLE:" Signs and symtoms; Allergies, medications, past pertinent medical history, last oral intake, events leading to accident).
  - **Assessment** – problem list.
  - **Plan** – plan for each problem and frequency in which you will monitor the patient.
        (from *SOLO Wilderness & Emergency Medicine.*)
- Improvise any needed splinting material. Foam pads work great.

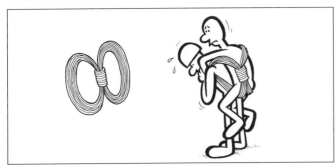

The split-rope carry.

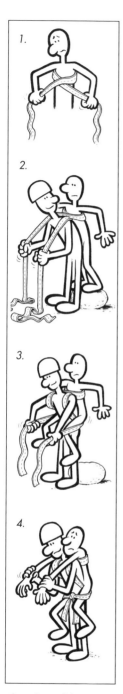

1.

2.

3.

4.

The nylon webbing
carry.

Transport the Victim

If necessary, transport the victim. A split-rope carry, fireman's carry or nylon webbing carry may be useful. A stretcher may be required to immobilize the victim and ease transport.

• While evacuating, continue to monitor the victim and record patient information at regular intervals.

Note: On many small, busy cliffs, the safest and fastest rescue technique is to simply yell for help. On a busy cliff, other climbers may be able to reach and assist the victim before the climbing partner can.

Note: The decision to transport a victim will be based on your level of first aid training. A victim who has sustained a potential head, neck, or spinal cord injury should be immobilized and transported by trained personnel with proper equipment.

The two-man rope carry.

The Complete Self-Rescue

This chapter takes you through an entire rescue, using only the skills that have been presented in this book thus far. An overview of a recommended sequence is provided, as well as a detailed description of each step.

THE SCENARIO

You are belaying a leader who falls near the top of a 150-foot pitch and breaks both ankles and wrists, but suffers no serious head or neck injuries. Your partner is in too much pain to safely belay and your remote location does not offer an opportunity to signal for help. You are seven pitches up a route that traverses a few pitches. Due to the nature of the route, it is very difficult to rappel the climb. If you can get to the top of this pitch with the victim, you can hike two-hundred yards across a very large ledge and rappel to the base of the climb. The rappel includes five full rope-lengths down a low-angled blocky slab. It is getting late, and you left your head lamps and extra clothing at the bottom of the route. Your partner is leading with two ropes.

Double Ropes

The leader's two ropes offer more rescue options. During the task analysis (presented below), the double-rope system is explained. The ropes are referred to as in the text and the illustrations as the White Rope and the Black Rope.

To avoid confusion:
- The White Rope is used for aid soloing/climbing with a Clove Hitch, as as a backup during the rescue.
- The Black Rope is used to ascend to the victim and establish the assisted hoist.

A RECOMMENDED SEQUENCE

The sequence that will be explained in detail in the task analysis follows:
- Ascend to the victim.
- Finish climbing the pitch to the ledge using a solo belay system.
- Descend the rope and unload/untie the bottom anchor.
- Haul the victim to the ledge.

  Note: Raising a victim is more difficult than lowering and is usually discouraged.

- Carry the victim to the rappel station.
- Conduct multiple assisted rappels with two ropes.

1.

the RESCUER
LOWERS the VICTIM
to a RELIABLE
PROTECTION POINT

the
RESCUER
HOLDS
the VICTIM'S
FALL.

STEP BY STEP

Ascend to the Victim

Begin by surveying the scene.

1. Lower the injured climber to the closest reliable piece of protection.
2. Escape the belay and anchor the ropes. Tie the victim off on the Black Rope using a Munter Mule knot and Figure Eight backup. Anchor the White Rope at its *end* with a Figure Eight to allow slack while ascending the rope.
3. Ascend the Black Rope to the victim. Assess the victim's injuries and administer first aid.
4. Backup the anchor that the victim has been lowered to and clip the victim to the anchor. Consider attaching a chest harness at this point.

Depending on your circumstances, you may prefer to re-establish your original belay anchor in the vicinity of the victim. At this point your original belay anchor is attaching one rope at its end and one rope is anchored with a Munter Mule Knot. Although re-establishing the anchor is much more time-consuming, it will allow you to complete the pitch using double ropes.

Note: While ascending, you will find quickdraws and protection points in place that may be under tension due to a traverse. Therefore, you may need to pass your ascending Prusiks around a carabiner. To do so, attach another Prusik above the carabiner and weight it. Next, untie the lower prusik.

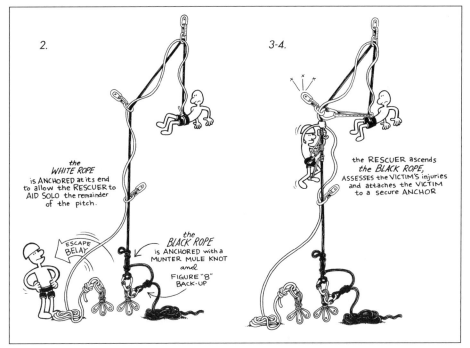

Aid/Free Climb the Pitch to the Ledge

The steps of a complete self rescue are illustrated above.

5. Attach a separate quickdraw to the anchor to which the victim is attached.
6. Take in all the slack on the White Rope so that it is taut on the lower anchor.
7. The White Rope is clipped through the new quickdraw and attached to the rescuer's harness using a Clove Hitch and locking carabiner – the same procedure described in the aid soloing chapter.
8. Untie the victim from the White Rope, pull the rope through the top anchor, and attach a backup Figure Eight to your harness – once again, the aid soloing procedure.
9. Using Prusiks, ascend the Black Rope to the top anchor. The White Rope should run through the Clove Hitch (as in aid soloing).
10 When you arrive at the top piece of protection, reinforce and build an anchor. This anchor must be *absolutely reliable*. It will need to hold the weight of the victim as well as a potential leader fall.
11. Clip a separate quickdraw to the anchor. Clip the White Rope through this quickdraw to aid solo/free climb utilizing the Clove Hitch tied to the White Rope.
12. When you arrive at the belay ledge, anchor the White Rope using a Munter Mule with a Figure Eight backup. Be extremely cautious of any edges or other areas that could damage the rope.

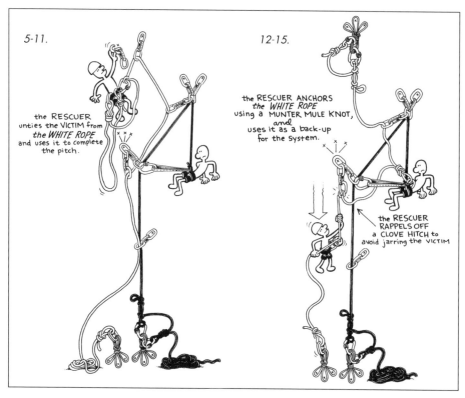

5-11.

12-15.

the RESCUER
unties the VICTIM from
the WHITE ROPE
and uses it to complete
the pitch.

the RESCUER ANCHORS
the WHITE ROPE
using a MUNTER MULE KNOT,
and
uses it as a back-up
for the system.

the RESCUER
RAPPELS OFF
a CLOVE HITCH to
avoid jarring the VICTIM

Descend and free the victim from the anchor

13. Rappel to the victim and clip yourself to the anchor.
14. Take four meters of slack from above the rappel device and tie a Figure Eight loop. Clip the victim to the loop – in the White Rope – to backup the rescue system.
15. Tie the White Rope to the anchor with a Clove Hitch and descend to the bottom anchor. The Clove Hitch should be tied so the victim is not tugged on by the descending rope.
16. When you reach the bottom, unload/untie the ropes from the anchors.

Haul the Victim to the Ledge

Note: You will be constructing an assisted hoist system and the Z-pulley system.

17. Ascend the White Rope and clean the pitch until you reach the victim.
18. Pass the victim as you continue to ascend the White Rope. Take in the slack from the Black Rope as you ascend.
19. Once you have reached the belay ledge, attach the Black Rope to the anchors using a Munter Mule combination with a Figure Eight backup. The Black Rope must be *taut* to the victim.

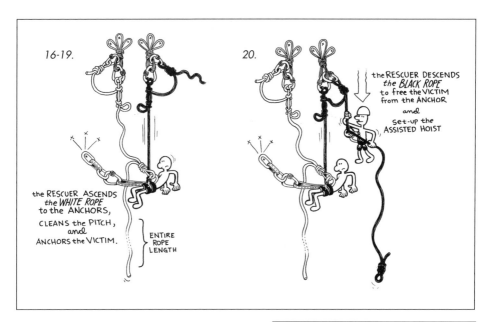

16-19.

the RESCUER ASCENDS
the WHITE ROPE
to the ANCHORS,

CLEANS the PITCH,
and
ANCHORS the VICTIM.

} ENTIRE
ROPE
LENGTH

20.

the RESCUER DESCENDS
the BLACK ROPE
to free the VICTIM
from the ANCHOR

and

Set-up the
ASSISTED HOIST

20. To backup your rappel, extend your rappel device and attach an Autoblock below your rappel device. Descend the Black Rope (you will be weighting the Figure Eight backup) to the victim and unclip him/her from the anchors.

21. To create a loop for the assisted hoist, clip the slack beneath the rappel device and Prusik through a locking carabiner attached to the front of the victim's harness. Take the other end of the rope with you as you again ascend.

   Note: If the victim is greater than a third of a rope-length away, you will be unable to arrange the assisted hoist.

22. Ascend the Black Rope to the anchors on the belay ledge. Clean the pitch as you ascend.

23. Pull in the slack from the loop that is running through the locking carabiner on the victim.

24. Create a Z-pulley on the slack portion of the loop. If the victim is able to assist in the hoist, the added advantage of the Z-pulley is probably not needed.

   Note: You have just created a 6:1 pulley. The 3:1 Z-pulley combines with the 2:1 pulley that is running through the locking carabiner on the victim's harness.

25. Haul the victim to the ledge.

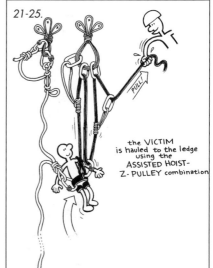

21-25.

PULL!

the VICTIM
is hauled to the ledge
using the
ASSISTED HOIST-
Z-PULLEY combination

Carry the Victim to the Rappel Station

26. Re-assess the victim's injuries and administer first aid, if needed.
27. Carry the victim to the rappel station.

Conduct Multiple Assisted Rappels

28. Utilize the Assisted Rappel, which is described in Chapter 7.
29. Once you have reached the ground, again assess the victim's injuries and the overall situation. Evacuate the victim or stabilize and locate assistance.

The mountains become melancholy with the loss of a fellow climber.

Photo: Jim Detterline

Appendix A

DEALING WITH A FATALITY

"From the moment the rope broke it was impossible to help them. So perished our comrades! For the space of half an hour we remained on the spot without moving a single step."
—Edward Whymper, *Scrambles Amongst The Alps*

The ultimate tragedy in the mountains is the accidental death of a companion. The overwhelming sense of loss and a deep feeling of helplessness can psychogenically paralyze the toughest survivors. However, even in a fatality scene there are certain chores that must be carried out to stabilize the scene, preserve the dignity of the deceased and aid the mental recovery of the survivors.

In a mountaineering death, the question that must be asked first is, "Is the scene is safe?" Is the rockfall, lightning hazard, avalanche danger or technical hazard stabilized? If not, take immediate action to direct the survivors to safety. Is it worth glissading down the same icy thousand-foot slope the victim just perished on, or is there an alternate route? Will the location of the victim place additional persons in deadly peril, or can the victim be safely approached? Look around and get the big picture before approaching the deceased person. Don't duplicate the accident.

In the United States, only a medical doctor or designee may officially pronounce death. The climber must be prepared to assess death, however, so that the energies of a rescue effort can be properly directed and good information can be relayed to the authorities. Certain signs of death may be obvious, especially if the deceased has been expired for some period of time. These may include rigidity of body tissues (rigor mortis occurs first in the jaw musculature in three to five hours), pooling of blood in body surfaces resting closest to the ground, algor mortis (the temperature of the body becomes ambient in eight to ten hours on the average), decomposition, decapitation and dismemberment. Greater difficulty arises in assessing a patient who is somewhere between loss of consciousness and biologic death (in which irreversible brain damage begins to occur), particularly if the patient has suffered some medical problem (such as a heart attack) as opposed to a traumatic injury.

You will have to examine the body, so glove up or wear plastic bags on your hands, especially if body fluids are exposed. Check first for respiratory arrest, looking for the rise and fall of the chest and air circulation from nose or mouth. Often, respiratory arrest is caused by a simple airway obstruction, such as the tongue falling back against the opening of the throat. Use your level of medical training to solve this if possible. Check other vital signs, such as pulse, blood pressure, central nervous system responses and pupillary response to light. Absence of pupillary response to light is a good indication that biologic death has occurred. When a person is dead, the pupils do not change size when light is shined at them, nor do the eyelids blink. The stare is glassy and vacant. Absence of pulse and breathlessness, however, may be solved through cardiopulmonary resuscitation (CPR). The training and certification required of CPR providers is generally inexpensive, requires a short time commitment and is a bare necessity for all climbers.

If you decide to administer mouth-to-mouth resuscitation, CPR or any other life-support measure, there may come a time when such measures must be discontinued due to no response or improvement from the patient. This is always a difficult decision. Most states permit certified emergency medical personnel to cease life support if they get too tired to carry on. Obviously, this is an important consideration if the rescuer is in the backcountry, far from any trailhead, telephone, or people who could assist or go for help.

Once it has been determined that a person is deceased, the scene of the accident must be preserved for the required investigations. In the United States, a death-scene investigator may be from a police department, sheriff's office, or National Park Service ranger unit. Other countries have similar public officials in charge of death investigations. In addition to the legal reasons for preserving a death scene, other purposes may include preventing bystanders from being traumatized and preserving clues that may help you and others understand why the accident happened and thus prevent similar occurrences.

Preserving a death scene is theoretically simple, but realistically difficult. First, separate the scene from the bystanders. The ideal way to do this is to cordon off a large area around and related to the fatality. Climbing ropes may be used to provide a physical barrier. If this is not possible, place a blanket or some other opaque covering over the body. Do not allow anyone without a legitimate reason into the area or to examine the body. Do not move the body from its resting position.

If possible, leave someone to guard the scene until the authorities arrive. Do not disturb fragile clues, such as footprints, other tracks, or placement of certain items (e.g. an ice ax stuck in the ice at the climber's high point). Sketch the scene, especially the position of the body and the placement of any fragile clues such as snow tracks. Photographs are very useful, but be prepared to turn all items over to the authorities. Make a note of the time and anything else that you remember as soon as possible, because your mind may later block these out. Don't let witnesses discuss what they saw with each other. Have them keep their testimony to themselves so it doesn't become tainted. If you have to leave a scene to get the authorities, leave a note on the body stating what happened, when it happened and that help is being summoned, so do not disturb. If you have to leave to summon help, take any valuables or identification from the body to give to the authorities .

Keep in mind that there may be other victims of a fatality scene. Those victims may include a survivor of the fatal event, a witness, a bystander, a family member or even an emergency service worker. Reach out to those people you think may be in need of an emotional crutch. Seek help yourself if you find you are a victim as well.

—JIM DETTERLINE

Climbing involves great risks and great beauty. Climb safely.

Jim Detterline photo

Appendix B

SOURCES

American Mountain Guides Association, *Guides Manual Alpine and Rock* (AMGA, 1992), p. "Munter Hitch," "Tying The Anchors Together."

American Mountain Guides Association (1996), ERNEST Anchor Description *Mountain Bulletin* IX(4), 7.

Tim J. Setnicka, *Wilderness Search and Rescue* (Boston: Appalachian Mountain Club, 1980), p. 175.

SOLO *Wilderness & Emergency Medicine,* Conway, NH.

RECOMMENDED READING

Bowman, Warren D. M.D. *Outdoor Emergency Care.* National Ski Patrol, System, Inc., 1988

Long, John. *How To Rock Climb.* Colorado: Chockstone Press, 1995.

Long, John. *How To Rock Climb: Climbing Anchors.* Colorado: Chockstone Press, 1993.

Long, John. *How To Rock Climb: More Climbing Anchors.* Colorado: Chockstone Press, 1996.

Long, John., John Middendorf *How To Rock Climb: Climbing Big Walls.* Colorado: Chockstone Press, 1994.

Luebben, Craig. *How To Rock Climb: Knots for Climbers.* Colorado: Chockstone Press, 1996.

March, Bill. *Rope Techniques in Mountaineering.* Police Square: Cicerone Press, 1992.

May, W.G. *Mountain Search and Rescue Techniques.* Boulder: Rocky Mountain Rescue Group Inc., 1973.

Peters, Ed, ed. *Mountaineering: The Freedom of the Hills.* Washington: The Mountaineers, 1982.

Selters, Andy. *Glacier Travel and Crevasse Rescue.* Seattle: The Mountaineers, 1990.

Strassman, Michael A. *Climbing Big Walls.* Indiana: ICS Books, 1990.

Setnicka, Tim J. *Wilderness Search and Rescue.* Boston: Appalachian Mountain Club, 1980.

RECOMMENDED ORGANIZATIONS

The organizations listed below should be able to direct you to classes on self-rescue.

American Mountain Guides Association: 710 10th Street, Suite 101, Golden Colorado 80401.

American Alpine Club, Inc.: 710 Tenth Street, Golden, CO 80401.

Mountain Rescue Association, Inc.: 200 Union Blvd., Suite 430-1355, Denver CO 80220.

SOLO Wilderness & Emergency Medicine; RFD 1, Box 163, Tasker Hill, Conway, NH 03818.

More Climbing Guides from Falcon and Chockstone Press

FALCON®